SOCIAL WORK NARRATIVES

SOCIAL WORK NARRATIVES

CAREER PATHWAYS and PRACTICE WISDOM

Hope Horowitz, MSW, LSW

Internet addresses given in this book were accurate at the time it went to press.

This book is intended as a reference volume only. The information given here is designed to inspire and inform.

Printed in the United States of America
Published in Hellertown, PA
Cover design by Christina Gaugler
Interior design by Suba Murugan

ISBN 978-1-958711-63-7

For more information or to place bulk orders, contact the author or the publisher at Jennifer@BrightCommunications.net.

Bright
COMMUNICATIONS

In Memory of Seth Michael Bloom

June 6, 1964–April 14, 2022

MSW: Yeshiva University Wurzweiler School of Social Work

BS: University of Delaware

Seth was the epitome of what it means to be a social worker. He embodied and modeled our social work values of service, social justice, dignity and worth of the person, importance of human relationships, integrity, and competence. He had the gift of being able to develop trusting relationships with everyone he encountered. He always had a smile to share, and he was able to guide difficult conversations using his leadership skills, empathy, compassion, and wisdom.

Seth had a deep commitment to the community and was an expert fundraiser. He spent his career working in various Jewish agencies, and he ran his own successful consulting business for thirteen years. His work focused mainly on nonprofit fundraising and large capital campaigns. He also used his expertise in the many volunteer leadership positions he held in local Jewish organizations. His passion, integrity, and advocacy skills allowed him to be a role model for everyone he encountered.

Seth was resilient as he dealt with brain cancer for eighteen years. Although social work was his career, it was his family that was most important to him and whom he loved dearly.

Contents

Introduction

Social workers like to help people. This is a common theme you will find when you ask someone why they want to be a social worker. Some people have had challenging life experiences and seek to change unfair systems and policies so others do not have to suffer. Others are attracted to social work because of the focus on social and economic justice and advocacy. And yes, we want to change the world!

I have taught Introduction to Social Work courses for many years. Each semester when I invite guest speakers to class to talk about their social work pathways and careers, students are mesmerized by their stories. We each have traveled a unique road as social work professionals. Learning about the variety of experiences helps students to see the myriad of opportunities available to social work professionals.

Social work is a unique profession that offers various pathways over a lifetime. No matter what path we take, social workers have knowledge, skills, and values in common. Our training is transferable to a variety of practice settings, enabling one to shift into different work environments throughout our career. Social work education provides us with the tools and knowledge we need to enhance people's lives and to make sure all people's basic human needs are met.

Historically, our roots are in working with vulnerable and oppressed populations. We work to empower people, advocate, and promote social and economic justice. We work with individuals, groups, families, organizations, and communities. Social work is about creating change both on the individual level and the societal level. We are critical thinkers. Our motto is to start where the client is at.

We value human diversity, respect human dignity, and are action oriented. We strive to be nonjudgmental and empathic while using a strengths perspective. Our approach uses a person in environment lens, meaning we look at the person and also the systems around that person impacting their life situation. We recognize how policies and laws impact our practice and ability to connect the people we serve with appropriate resources.

Social workers follow the National Association of Social Workers (NASW) Code of Ethics requiring us to practice by upholding the six values of the profession as our guide, which are *service, social justice, dignity and worth of the person, importance of human relationships, integrity, and competence.* We live by these values both professionally and personally. These core values form the foundation for our unique purpose and perspective and guide us to make ethical decisions with those we serve. We also value confidentiality, autonomy, self-determination and setting clear boundaries. Our own self-awareness is key. These values and perspectives are the hallmark of our profession.

As you read the pages of this book, seek to be inspired by the stories while also thinking about yourself and your passions. Each person in this book has been a part of my life during the more than forty two years I have been a social worker. I had the pleasure of interviewing each of them asking a series of thought-provoking questions about what it means to be a social worker. Pondering the questions allowed each of us to reflect on our careers.

I hope you will enjoy meeting these mentors, former students, and colleagues of mine. You will meet retired social workers and others at various points in their career. Each story you read provides a glimpse into the twists and turns of career pathways in social work. Watch for common themes that emerge as you read the stories. Look for a story or stories that inspire you.

If you are new to social work, know you have many opportunities that await. If you are seeking to move to a new practice setting, see how others have made the change. I encourage you to learn from the practice wisdom you will find as part of each story. While we can learn from textbooks, professional articles, and writing papers, the wisdom developed through practice is invaluable. You will also find advice about self-care and the importance of incorporating self-care into your daily life.

At the end of the book are questions to prompt your thinking about what you want out of a social work career and how to achieve your vision. Keep in mind that while you might see a path unfolding, it's important to take note of opportunities that present themselves along your social work journey that you might not have thought about. The challenge is recognizing the opportunities! Be inspired! Be the change!

I Knew I Wanted to Be a Social Worker

Jenna Sawicki, LSW

MSW: Marywood University

BSW: Cedar Crest College

Social Work Pathway and Work Experience

I was an avid reader as a child and read a lot of books that had social workers in the story. I remember watching a show called *Judging Amy* that included a social worker who worked with children. I thought, *That sounds like a nice job.*

Jenna Sawicki, LSW

But in high school, teachers told me it was not a good profession to go into because you don't make any money. After graduating from high school, I went to Northampton Community College (NCC) and thought, *Let me take a social work class so I can figure out if this is what I want.*

When I took the class, I knew I was going to go further and become a social worker. While I was a student at NCC, I participated in a service trip to help rebuild after Hurricane Katrina devastated areas in New Orleans. This experience helped me understand the pieces of social work where I could be creating change in a social justice context. After getting my Associate in Social Work degree at NCC, I transferred to Cedar Crest College for a BSW. Because I had advanced standing having earned a BSW, I was able to get my MSW at Marywood University in one calendar year.

For my MSW internship, I was placed in the emergency room at Sacred Heart Hospital in Allentown, Pennsylvania. I remember being in the psychiatric unit one day, when I had to call a patient's family to get the psychosocial. I was talking to the mom the way I would talk to anyone. She stopped me and said, "I just want to say I'm so happy that there's someone like you who's talking to my daughter and helping her." All I thought was, *I can't believe that. How are people talking to patients?* I was just listening and being empathic. I realized these are important social work skills not everyone possesses.

My first job after getting my MSW was at Providence Community Services. Because I did not have work experience, I began as Therapeutic Support Staff (TSS). Once I gained some experience, I moved up to become a Mobile Behavioral Therapist working with children with developmental disabilities. This involved going into children's homes or schools to develop behavioral plans and provide therapy. I worked there for about five years.

My next job was at Women's Resources, an agency that deals with domestic violence and sexual assault. I worked there for ten years, beginning as a child advocate, and also working with some adults. Part of the job was answering the twenty-four-hour hotline. Due to government funding, most roles were either domestic violence or sexual assault, but I handled both. I was part of the sexual assault response team, and sometimes I went to the hospital to support the victim. As a child advocate, I worked with kids in schools, and they also came to my office at the agency. I was promoted to Senior Counselor, and I oversaw the other counselors, but I still saw clients.

These were taxing jobs. For example, when you respond to a sexual assault at the hospital, you are sitting with people in some of their worst moments. Women's Resources also has a thirty-day emergency shelter for emergency violent situations. Due to a lack of resources in the community, clients might extend their stay to gain some time to find new housing. Thirty days was usually not enough time to get housing. I was able to do this work for ten years only because I changed roles and moved up in the organization. It was difficult work.

One story that stands out to me was going to court with one of my first clients. She was going to court for a protection from abuse (PFA). Her mom and I sat with her the whole time. Her soon-to-be ex-husband was also there, and he had his whole family in the courtroom trying to intimidate her. She was so thankful I was there to sit with her and support her.

When I decided to look for a new job, I became interested in working with kidney dialysis patients. I was hired at DaVita Dialysis as a dialysis social worker. I work at two clinics with patients concerning psychosocial needs, help to get people on the transplant list, conduct mental health screenings, provide help with insurance, and fill out surveys sent from the state. I help patients adjust to being on dialysis and understand dialysis, which is a process that usually takes three to four and a half hours and removes and flushes toxins from the kidneys. I enjoy working with the patients and helping them feel comfortable. It is not a job that you take home with you because it is not something that happened because of what someone else did. The person's kidney is simply not functioning correctly. This is much different than working in domestic violence. I have been doing this job about three years so far, and I really enjoy what I am doing. It is a well-paying job, and the hours are flexible. There are no evenings, and I do not take the work home!

Self-Care Tips

Before I had my twin girls, I would go to yoga. I did not like to spend a lot of money on myself, and I had one supervisor who said, "You should never question investing in yourself."

I thought, *She's right.* That was the first time someone ever told me it's okay to take care of yourself, and that was a valuable lesson.

Practice Wisdom and Advice

- Follow your gut. For example, if your work environment is toxic, it is time to do something else. If you are always tired from your work, question if that is the right place for you and don't be afraid to make a change.

- Consider other options. When you are looking for a new job, don't be afraid to apply even if you would be changing settings. Know you can use your social work skills in many different practice settings. Because social work is versatile, there are many different options where you can work.
- Capitalize on opportunities that come your way. I realized how much I love service, volunteering, and actively helping people when I went on the New Orleans trip. In 2019, I was asked to be one of the mentors on the NCC Mindful Travel Mentors trip to Finland that included social work professionals, faculty, and social work students. I enjoyed being a mentor to students, learning about the social service organizations in Finland, and understanding why Finland is the happiest place in the world.

Final Thoughts

As a social worker in the Monroe County area of the Pocono Mountains, Pennsylvania, I find the lack of social systems and resources challenging. For instance, transportation is a major problem. There really is no reliable public transportation, and ride shares are expensive and do not go to certain areas. People struggle just to live, and there is a five-year waiting list for the housing authority. The availability of shelters is inadequate. I think there is a problem with services in many locations. It is frustrating when you are trying to help clients and cannot connect them with appropriate resources.

What I love most about being a social worker is helping people in the moment as much as I can. I always tell them I don't have all the answers, but I will help them to the best of my ability. Even if their questions seem small, I always try my best to be as kind as possible.

Self-Care, Self-Awareness, and Becoming a Relationship Specialist

Aliya Kenyatta, LCSW

MSW: Marywood University

BA: Temple University

Social Work Pathway and Work Experience

Ever since I was in high school, I knew I wanted to be some type of therapist because I like taking things apart, seeing how they work, and then putting them back together in a more efficient way. I determined that was the route I wanted to take, but I wasn't sure what that road was going to look like. I just knew that was the end goal.

Aliya Kenyatta, LCSW, Relationship Specialist

At first, I thought about child psychology and counseling. I went to Temple University in Philadelphia with the thought of becoming a trilingual social psychologist. The first semester, I dropped Spanish as a minor. I was taking sociology courses as a minor, but it wasn't connecting for me, so I dropped that too. I loved psychology, but from my perspective it was a little too white male focused. It wasn't for me.

My father is an African studies professor, and I thought, *Why couldn't I get a degree in African American studies?* I fought some limiting beliefs I had about that degree and realized it was the path I wanted to take. I majored in African American studies and minored in psychology. I graduated in 2012 at the height of the recession when everybody was struggling to find jobs.

After my college graduation, I moved back to the Poconos, Pennsylvania, and started working as a secretary in the counseling department at Northampton Community College (NCC). The stars had aligned because I was around counseling. I wasn't doing exactly what I wanted to do, but it was nice to be around counselors. I had the chance to ask counselors questions like, "If you were to go back, what would you do?" and "What would you change about your path?"

Many said they would choose social work. In high school, I had done a career assessment that said I should be a social worker. I remember thinking, *Oh, no, I don't want to do that.* I had no idea what social work was other than what they show on the media—stereotypical social work. Once I got the opinions from the counselors, I started looking into social work. My mother also worked at NCC, and when I told her I was interested in social work, she connected me with author Hope Horowitz, who connected me to Dr. Lyter at Marywood University's MSW Pocono program. After that, everything just flowed. I met with Dr. Lyter, and it seemed like the right place to be. It fit into my life schedule because I was able to go to classes on Saturdays and still care for very young twin daughters. Being a single mother, it was challenging to find time to fit in an internship. I did both internships at NCC in two different areas, and it worked out well for me.

When I graduated with my MSW, I was invited to an event where directors of counseling departments got together. I met the Director of Counseling Services at Muhlenberg College in Allentown, Pennsylvania, who said that there was an open fellowship. He told me the pay and I remember thinking it was so low, I would not be able to survive on that. My colleague convinced me to apply and said, "Even if you have to cut back on some things, I think it is very worth it for you to take this fellowship and see what comes from it. The connections you will make will be worth it." I took the fellowship, and I'm very thankful I did.

I was offered a full-time position at Muhlenberg College in Allentown, Pennsylvania. I started right before the COVID-19 pandemic and have been there ever since! We counselors at Muhlenberg do clinical customized care, which puts us in a more clinical mindset. Every student is prescribed a certain number of sessions based on what is clinically necessary and appropriate for them. For example, one student might need one appointment, while others might need five. Some might need supportive ongoing therapy, but we like to separate the difference between supportive therapy versus clinical, which can be difficult because people are used to private–practice type therapy when you can go weekly and go on and on. Using the clinical customized care approach means we ask the student, "What are your therapeutic goals right now?" For example, goals may be decreasing anxiety, working on friendships, relationships, etc. Once the student has met that goal, we end the counseling and always let the student know they can come back to work on another goal. It is included in their health and wellness fee, making it easy to get assistance.

When the pandemic happened, we had to quickly transition to working on Zoom and provide therapy for students at the same time we were experiencing our own trauma. There was a lot of parallel processing. We had to change to an emergent type of model because so many students were in different states, and we could not provide therapy over state lines. We did more consultation to help students deal with the pandemic. Currently, we offer in-person and telehealth sessions. I work on campus with one day remote.

My specialty is relationships. I love all relationships. It's my thing. I'm very much known as the "relationship person" on campus! I also work for a private practice and enjoy that as well.

Self-Care Tips

I credit the Director of the Counseling Center at Muhlenberg College because he models and structures self-care in a realistic way. Self-care is integrated into our daily life. We don't start seeing students until 9:00 am, but we arrive by 8:30 am so we have time to relax and catch up on notes. We also have designated administrative time, so we are not rushing in to see student after student. That's also not good for therapy. We have lunch blocked out from 12 to 12:30 pm, and because we really enjoy being together we eat together, which helps break up the day. We are encouraged to see about five clients per day. The director shared research that says seeing more than five people a day results in a decline, and you are not doing your best work. This reminds us how important it is to take care of ourselves first. If we are feeling burned out, our department culture encourages us to take a walk, or a quick nap, or do something so you can recharge. This goes against conventional thinking and typical belief systems, and it works! We also take care of each other and notice if someone is a little off. Maybe that person needs to go home or work remotely that day.

We supervise interns from various graduate schools and teach them the mentality and importance of taking care of oneself. We empower them to go into old thinking environments and learn how to advocate for themselves and even try to change the old culture.

Practice Wisdom and Advice

- Explore limiting beliefs. Really understand the beliefs you have about yourself in social work, what you've been taught, and what you've heard about social workers. While you're learning how to be a social worker, you can see them kind of just melting away and be *consciously aware* as this happens. Also, explore your limiting beliefs around specialties.
- Incorporate yourself into your work. You don't have to become a social work robot. You were a full person before you went into social work. Ask yourself, *What is unique about me that I bring to my work with the client?* Being genuine and authentic is important so you don't have imposter syndrome.
- Don't feel trapped. Social work is versatile and empowering. If you need to make a change, you can go in so many different

directions. Social work is broad because you literally can work from birth until death with any type of population in any type of environment.

- When it comes to pricing and charging clients in private practice, I think my rates are fair, but many social workers undervalue themselves. I think the mindset is "I want to keep myself accessible to clients." I believe you really have to question whether or not that's sustainable. I charge what I need to make enough money to live. Now that I'm secure, I can give pro bono sessions and offer a sliding scale.

Final Thoughts

The most challenging part of social work for me has been fighting the glorification of burnout. The helping professions tend to have a culture of "how much of myself can I sacrifice but also take care of everyone else?"

When it comes to salary, people say, "I didn't get into this field to make money." I do not agree. I don't like that stereotype, which continues to permeate throughout the profession, and I've actively worked to try to fight that because it completely goes against my philosophy. I believe you must take care of yourself first. If I am not okay, it is hard to care for others. When I became a social worker, I had that mindset specifically when it comes to salary because I am a single mother of two, and I need to make sure that I'm well first. The pandemic highlighted my belief that I have to be well to take care of my clients.

When I walked into social work, I felt like it was made for my personality. I started understanding what it means to work on a micro level and advocate on the macro level. That is exactly what I do.

Having a background in African American studies has been very helpful in shaping how I view social work and allowing the social work profession to work for me and me to work for it. African American studies gave me the understanding of what problems exist, and social work has given me the tools to be able to help fix them.

A Career in Child Welfare

Lisa Hand, LSW

MSW: Marywood University

BA: Moravian University

Social Work Pathway and Work Experience

My undergraduate degree was from Moravian College (now University), and I majored in elementary education to become a teacher. But when I graduated, not many teaching jobs were available. I wound up subbing, then permanent subbing, but I couldn't find a permanent job. I did that for about a year and a half, and it was tough.

Lisa Hand, LSW

Then one of my friends asked, "Did you ever think about child welfare? I know somebody who works for the county, and it's more money." It was also a permanent position, which is really what I wanted. I took a Civil Service test and got the lowest-level job called a Caseworker Trainee. I was a trainee for maybe six months and then became a Caseworker. I went from Caseworker to Supervisor to Program Specialist and eventually was promoted to Program Director during my twenty-eight-year career!

Each job change came at a time when I was starting to feel burned out and needed a new challenge. In child welfare, you hear a lot of the same things over and over and you get a lot of resistance. Most of the parents we work with are not willing partners, so to speak. They're mandated to work with us, so working through a lot of resistance hostility is a part of the job. The direct service wears on you.

I decided to get an MSW through a collaborative program the county participated in that was funded by the state and federal government called Child Welfare Education for Leadership (CWEL). The program was designed to keep people in child welfare because it is a difficult field to stay in long term. Our agency offered one spot a year. It was competitive, and I had to apply and interview.

I was accepted! The CWEL program provided me with 95 percent of my salary, and I did not have to work during the two years in graduate school. I went to Marywood University. At the time, I was in a lower-level administration job, but I knew I wanted to move up. I decided to take the administrative track that had general social work courses but also courses where I could learn skills such as grant writing, supervision, working with boards, and organizational leadership.

I was fortunate to have my internship with the administrator of our agency, who was there more than thirty years, and he knew so much. I always admired him, and he was a very ethical person. He really allowed me to see what an administrator does and took me to regional and state meetings to help give me the big picture of what an administrator role includes.

He said, "If you want to move up to this type of position, this is what you'll be doing, and this is how you manage decisions."

When we met for supervision, he would give me a situation and say, "This is the problem. What would you do?" So, I had to think about it and give an answer.

Then he would say, "Well, then, this is going to happen. You're dealing with a lot of different pieces. You're not just dealing with people you supervise. You're also dealing with the union, the public, and the media, and you have to juggle it all."

He allowed me to see the administrative world firsthand, and I knew that was where I wanted to be.

Earning my MSW helped me move up to a higher administrative position, which was my goal. When you are in child welfare administration, you are not providing the actual direct service, but you still hear the terrible stories and must make important decisions concerning children's and families' lives as you lead your team.

Self-Care Tips

I waited until I retired to really integrate self-care into my life. Self-care was not always something I did regularly. I might exercise and enjoy it, but I did not do it on a routine basis. Sometimes I would get home, I would think about a case that really touched my heart, and I just could not get it out of my mind. I learned it is wise to cut yourself off when you leave work. There is a system in place that takes over after you leave that office. So let that happen. When I retired, it probably took around six months for the stress to finally leave my body. My sleep was better, and everything seemed to feel better in my life.

When you're doing that daily grind, you might not realize how stressed you are, and I probably should have done something to release the stress. Sometimes other people notice you are stressed before you do. If somebody asks, "Is everything okay? Are you feeling stressed?" think about that and tell yourself, "I need to step back and recognize how I am feeling and what is going on for me" so you are dealing with the problem and not taking it out on others.

Practice Wisdom and Advice

- You certainly need to have a passion for your job because there's not necessarily a lot of perks such as pay and schedule. If you feel you shouldn't be in a job you are in, it is time to move on. You have to ask yourself, "Is this really what I am looking for and enjoy doing?" Maybe you need a different area of social work practice. Do your research and talk to people in that area. As a social worker, you must know somebody in a different area whom you could ask,

"What's this job like? What would I be doing? How would I go about my day?" Make the move so you are happy in your position and can feel passionate about your job.

- Take the ethics part of your job very seriously. I know when you're getting a social work degree, they weave ethics into everything, every class. It is the most important thing to learn. I still go back to the Code of Ethics for guidance if I'm struggling with something. It might clear up what I need to do, or I might need to do further research on an issue. Ethical behavior must be part of your daily practice.
- Always think of the dignity and worth of a person no matter what—even if a person you're working with might be different from you, abrasive to you, or combative with you. You have to start at ground zero with the dignity of that person and treat them with respect.

Final Thoughts

Supervision is important. In child welfare, I think the supervisory positions are the most important positions. I supervised five caseworkers as a first-level supervisor. In any agency, you look to your supervisor, whether it's consciously or unconsciously, to learn the culture, boundaries, and how to do things properly. Supervisors need to set expectations and guidelines and make clear what ethical and unethical behavior looks like. Supervisors set the tone.

In child welfare, you must follow federal and state guidelines, and those guidelines are there for a reason. You can have different types of supervisors, some who lead by example and others who are lax and don't handle things that should be dealt with. I was fortunate to have great supervisors, and I tried to model what I was taught with those I supervised.

One of the challenges I had as a caseworker was in the adoption unit, trying to unite children with their families. By the time a case came to the adoption unit, most options had been tried and failed, and now we are obligated by law to move toward termination of parental rights. I think the hardest thing is knowing you worked with that parent and got as far as the termination process. There was no doubt they loved their child, they cared for them, and they didn't want their rights to be terminated. The parent might have had their own trauma in life growing up and might not have gotten help or might have lacked support. That was the most difficult thing I dealt with.

A highlight of my career was the job of Program Director, which I retired from. I was responsible for running more than one-third of the agency. When I retired, I was one of the senior people for length of service to CYS. I enjoyed working with my team and staff, collaborating in the community and with other agencies, as well as finding ways to streamline processes. I loved when new ideas unfolded so I never felt stagnant.

Service, Living Your Dreams, and Being Humble

Jennifer Bruno, LCSW

MSW: Marywood University

BSW: Cedar Crest College

Social Work Pathway and Work Experience

When I was a child, my family relocated from the Bronx, New York, to Bethlehem, Pennsylvania. In middle school, I got into some trouble by being rebellious, so I was assigned mandatory community service. That's when my love for social work began.

Jennifer Bruno, LCSW

I did not know that "social work" was what it was called until I went to high school. In order to graduate, we needed to complete community service, which I loved. While studying at Northampton Community College, I went on a trip to New Orleans to rebuild homes after Hurricane Katrina. I recognized that was also service. I realized I could major in social work and get paid to do something I loved, which was exciting.

I received my Associate Degree in Social Work from Northampton Community College, then I transferred to Cedar Crest College for two years, earning my bachelor's in social work (BSW). I then earned my MSW from Marywood University in one year because of advanced standing.

I have had an interesting social work journey. I did my BSW internship at Northampton County Children and Youth, which was quite an experience. It was a good way to get into the social work field and the community and see the issues people face. My MSW internship was at Valley Youth House, which is an agency that works primarily with vulnerable, abused, and homeless youth. After completing my internship, I was hired and started working for the Family Intervention Program and the Functional Family Therapy Program, which focused on in-home family counseling and families who struggled with drugs, alcohol, and family issues. After working there for about three years, I decided I wanted to change jobs and do something different.

I went to hospice and was a medical social worker. Going from working with youth and families struggling with addiction to working with people struggling with chronic illnesses and end of life was a big difference! Working in hospice was wonderful. I loved it. It was interesting to see the role of a medical social worker, and I learned a lot about the medical and aging sides of social work, but also the grieving and bereavement process. That worked out for a while, but my job required me to be on call. This was challenging as I was starting a family.

After that, I worked at a Federally Qualified Health Center (FQHC) known as Neighborhood Health Center of Lehigh Valley. This agency primarily serves people who have little to no health insurance. Once again, I was in the medical field, working with doctors and other professionals but serving on the behavioral health side. We offered short-term therapy to families who scored positive or scored high on their behavioral assessments. After they completed short-term counseling, we would discharge and/or refer them to higher levels of care in the community.

Then the COVID-19 pandemic happened, giving us the option to work from home. I loved being accessible to my children. When it was time to go back to working in the office, I wanted to stay home. Eventually, I got a part-time job working for someone else's private practice and was able to leave the clinic and work full-time private practice. After working there full-time for two years, I have recently returned to part time in order to open my own private practice, Fruitful Seeds Counseling, LLC, located in Bethlehem, Pennsylvania. I am a bilingual Licensed Clinical Social Worker able to work with a variety of diverse clients. In the future, I look forward to supervising social work interns and mentoring them as they find their path. My practice focuses on mental health, families and individuals, couples, and helping those with substance use disorders. I accept most insurances. I have some private pay clients, and I offer a sliding scale fee for people who can't afford the cost for visits. I work with a third party that helps with credentialing and recruiting so I can focus on the therapy.

One highlight of my work was when I worked with a hospice patient who was a mother at the end stage of her life. For years and years, there was a lot of discord with the son because of his sexual orientation. Through our meetings, education, and support, I was able to provide a moment of reconciliation with them before she passed.

Another highlight was when I worked at the medical clinic. I spent a lot of time working with an immigration attorney, which was interesting. Being Spanish speaking and able to serve that population, I felt honored when people trusted me with their stories of being immigrant refugees or applying for asylum. In a lot of cases, I was able to work with the attorney to help them obtain a "U nonimmigrant visa," which was necessary if they were trying to escape physical or mental abuse. We would vouch for why they shouldn't return to their country, and they could be granted permission to be here.

Most challenging has been working as a social worker in the medical world and finding some professionals don't look at social work as valuable, as equally important as what they do, or they do not listen to you as much. I take courage and confidence that what social

Grow through what you go through and you don't have to do it alone.

workers bring to the table is important—often things other professionals miss, overlook, or don't take into consideration.

Often it can be hard to get the credit you feel you earn at the table. However, there are also many medical professionals who value what you have to say because they are not used to seeing situations from a social work perspective.

Self-Care Tips

Recognizing your strength might also be your limitation. Making self-care a regular practice is so important to prevent burnout.

I feel it's so easy to overwork or overcommit when helping others comes naturally. You could do it all day every day, and it doesn't feel like a job. For me, self-care includes disconnecting from my phone when I'm not working, not checking emails, or not responding immediately.

Because I'm in front of the computer and inside a lot for work, I find spending time outside in nature helps me practice being in the moment and mindfulness.

Sometimes I just practice stillness. Can I sit still for five minutes with my thoughts and feelings? We are constantly checking in on everyone else, so can I just not do anything and be okay with that even for five minutes?

Practice Wisdom and Advice

- Foster empathy, compassion, and the ability to meet people where they are. Some people might not be ready or willing to change or work on things, and admitting there's a problem can often be scary stuff. When a client simply shows up, it can be a huge start and many times a huge step because they are acknowledging something might be wrong.
- Stay humble. I value staying humble and simple because I always feel honored people entrust me with their confused/conflicted minds and/or their broken hearts. We might be the professional helping or leading them, but they are the experts of their stories.
- Don't let anyone discourage you from your dreams.

Final Thoughts

I have learned that a lot of social workers come into social work not because of the money, but because of the heart, wanting to help people, to change people's lives. Sometimes it's because of our own chaos we grew up with or the things that we couldn't change in our own lives. What makes you a good professional is taking the time to work on "your own stuff." You start to become more self-aware and insightful of yourself, others, and the process of healing.

Little girls with dreams become Women of Vision.

It is important to look for mentors. I tended to gravitate toward students who were older and already had life experience. I watched them and listened to them because I always felt like I was the youngest, so I always had so much to learn. In the workplace, I valued learning from my coworkers and supervisors, even if they were not social workers.

I think supervision is critical because no matter how long we have been doing this, we can always gain different perspectives. Always ask for guidance so you can stay sharp. If you don't have supervision, consider how you can check to make sure you are being ethical and maybe consider doing something differently.

If you chose social work, you probably have a lot of compassion and empathy. Maybe sometimes you'll be discouraged by others about pay or asking, "Why would you want to do that?" I really do believe when you love what you do and you do it well, the opportunities come to you, and you will advance quickly. Don't be discouraged by what others say or think.

I wish that when I was going through school going to counseling would have been a requirement. We must consider how much of our own stuff we have not dealt with before we start dealing with other people's stuff. If students can get counseling on their own just to make sure they're okay and see what it feels like to be on the other side, we will be better equipped and be better professionals.

If you are a brand-new student figuring out what to do in social work, know it's a versatile field with many options. If you are already in the profession for a while and you want to do something else, be open-minded and try new things to figure out if "this is for me, or this is not for me, this population works, this age doesn't work." There's no right way or wrong way to do it. It's all a process of trial and error as you continue to find your purpose. Personally and professionally, I wish you well as you continue to grow through what you go through!

A Different Social Work Pathway

Jonathan Picker, LCSW

MSW: University of Pittsburgh

BA: University of Pittsburgh

Social Work Pathway and Work Experience

As an undergraduate, I majored in anthropology and participated in a "Semester at Sea Voyage." When I was finishing my degree, I knew I had to get a master's degree. At the time, I was not a hundred percent sold on anthropology as my career path.

Jonathan Picker, LCSW

I thought about social work and decided to get my MSW. One of the reasons I chose social work was because I knew even back at age twenty that I would always have a job. It would be lifetime employability.

I had to pick a concentration, and at that time the options were community and organizations, therapy, and administration. I picked administration because I wanted to be an administrator. When I started and enrolled in classes I didn't see my advisor until halfway into the semester, so I had to pick classes on my own. I went through the catalog and picked some random courses that seemed interesting. The random classes that I ended up taking were all models of treatment such as group therapy and family dynamics. When I went and met my advisor for the first time, she basically told me that the majority of the four courses I was taking would not fulfill the course requirements for the administrative track. I had two choices. I could switch my concentration or keep going and use the courses as electives. I switched the concentration to the therapeutic side and models of treatment. That became my focus. Pitt had a lot of funding and grants for children and youth services, so I picked the children and youth specialty within the therapy concentration.

When I graduated, my wife and I moved to North Carolina. My first job was for the Wake County Alcohol Treatment Center, where I conducted drug and alcohol assessments. I also did treatment and ran lectures and small groups. That was my introduction to understanding other people's experiences because I was tested constantly. Clients would ask, "Are you a drug addict? Are you in recovery?"

I learned very quickly from some savvy therapists that this was a trap question. If I said, "No, I am not in recovery," which I'm not, then they would assume I don't know what they're talking about or experiencing. From that experience, I learned it doesn't matter if I walked in the same shoes as another person. I live a sober life. I have information that I can give to you, but it's up to you to take it or not. That was my introduction to social work practice.

After a couple of years in North Carolina, my wife and I moved to Philadelphia to be closer to family and friends. I worked for a community mental health center in the northeastern part of Philly with patient populations with dual diagnoses. I did therapy and had all types of patients, including psychopathic and borderline bipolar patients. Other visitors just came in every week because they had nothing better to do and just wanted to visit with me for an hour. I learned quite a bit from that experience, making me a better therapist.

At the time, what I really wanted to figure out was how I could be a social worker and help people, and make as much money as possible. My solution was to work in managed care. The bulk of my career since 1998 has been in managed care. I've worked for United Behavioral Health and Aetna. I have done concurrent reviews for inpatient hospitalizations, working with providers authorizing ongoing treatment, making sure patients were getting what they needed, understanding benefit designs, and explaining to parents why they should send their kid to three months or six months of long-term residential or why they should not. We were looking for ways to help people understand that managed care wasn't designed to say no to a service. Managed care seeks the most appropriate service with the least restrictive containment to address patient needs.

In 2017, my story shifted. I had some unexpected experiences. An opportunity opened at a company working with primary care physicians and data analytics, looking at patients' medical conditions and population health. That is really my specialty. After working at that company for two years, I lost my job. I was unemployed for three months and had subsequent jobs as a behavioral health consultant and healthcare advocate at Optum. I lost that job because it went overseas. I went through a couple of periods of unemployment.

Right before the COVID-19 pandemic started, I got a job at Jefferson Health University System as a behavior health specialist, blended with two primary care physicians. My referrals came only from those PCP offices. If a patient went to see their PCP for an annual physical or for a sick visit, they were asked questions such as, "Do you have any problems with sleep or appetite? Do you feel anxious?" Depending on the responses, the PCP would refer the patient to me for a mental health assessment, after which I might meet with them for subsequent sessions, or refer out.

This was during the COVID-19 pandemic, and telehealth was new. It was kind of shaky for the first month, but once they got telehealth up and running, it ran well. I had worked mostly with adults in my career, but telehealth opened the opportunity for me to work with teens and some geriatric patients as well. I left Jefferson when they began talking about returning to the offices under a hybrid model. I knew I didn't want to be in a primary care office where I would have to wear a gown, mask, and shield.

Currently, I work at Optum on their quality field operations team and work with a group of primary care physicians. I work with the quality folks to identify which patients need tests such as mammograms and colonoscopies. I do chart reviews and presentations with the providers on how they're doing against where they should be month over month. I try to get them to a four-star or better rating. For every wellness visit where doctors receive at least three-and-a-half stars, they receive quarterly incentive checks. At the end of the year, they receive a payment based on overall performance.

This type of work might sound a bit different than the typical social work world, but it's an opportunity to do social work services in the business climate. For me, it was a way to use my social work skills and my social work experience.

Self-Care Tips

Self-care is important. I listen to music. I also watch comedies, and I've been rewatching *The Office, Family Guy,* and silly comedian shows just to laugh.

I exercise and go for walks. I like to go out to eat. I enjoy talking to old friends.

Early in my career, I felt the weight of the world and realized the importance of not taking my work home.

Practice Wisdom and Advice

- Get your license early in your career. Don't wait! It is a good idea to get a clinical license, even if you do not plan to do clinical work, because you never know how your career might unfold and opportunities that might open to you because of the clinical license.
- When you have an opportunity to get a credential, do it!
- Be an advocate, not only for your clients but for yourself. As social workers, we do not get paid what we are worth. Our profession is highly specialized and credentialed, yet our pay does not always reflect the work we do.
- Treat everybody as you want to be treated.
- Pay attention to language. I learned this lesson early on in my career. I was on a call with a provider, and it was an alcohol treatment facility. The patient was on a mental health unit but was getting detox because they came in drunk and suicidal. The patient was placed on a dual

diagnosis unit. I asked the provider, "What are we going to do about the alcohol use?" The provider responded, "We are the treatment team, not you."

It became an adversarial conversation because I used "we," making it sound like I was part of the team. I was on some level, but the provider felt I was only respecting myself when I'm the insurance company and not the treatment team. How we frame things and the language we use with clients and our patients is critical to establish the relationship. If you don't have the relationship, you have nothing. Words matter.

Final Thoughts

I have not encountered many male social workers, and that is the one challenge I have had. I have always been aware that my supervisors have been female. I would like to see more male social workers. I think there is a good deal of gender stereotyping of who a social worker is. I would like to encourage more young males to become social workers to create more balance in the profession.

I was a lousy therapist in my twenties because I didn't have the experience. I dealt with a lot of couples and adults. I tried to pay attention and do the best I could with the skills I had. I once worked with a hoarder, and I didn't know much about hoarding. I also had a pure sociopath who, after the third session, clearly didn't want to be there, but he was mandated to see me. He looked right through me and scared the heck out of me. As I have gotten older, and especially once I hit fifty, my view of the world completely changed. I've had more experience in different areas, allowing me to be more effective with clients. It's fine to be young and energetic and provide therapy, but I believe experience makes a big difference.

I know I couldn't be anywhere without having the MSW degree even in these more business-focused environments. An MSW is a diverse, versatile degree that allows you to go in many directions throughout your career.

Relationships, Being "Real," and Discovering a Passion for Social Work

Lauren Heydt, LSW

MSW: University of Pennsylvania

BSW: Kutztown University of Pennsylvania

Social Work Pathway and Work Experience

My social work journey began during my time at Kutztown University, where I initially aspired to become a kindergarten teacher. However, as I started taking education classes, I realized that my enthusiasm for the courses was lacking. I yearned for a major that would lead me to a job that I was truly passionate about and thoroughly enjoyed. It was during my research on the difficulties students face in their learning that I came across Maslow's Hierarchy of Needs. This discovery ignited a deep desire within me to work with the most challenging students, those who were considered "unreachable" by others.

Lauren Heydt, LSW

My path to becoming a social worker was influenced by my own personal experiences. The truth is I endured abuse during my childhood and longed for someone to confide in. While my teachers and the school counselor were supportive, I yearned for someone whom I could truly pour my heart out to and receive the help I desperately needed. This led me to wonder if I could be that person for someone else, someone who could change their perspective of themselves and help them find true happiness.

I remember my father, who is both my role model and best friend, taking me out to dinner to discuss my interest in majoring in social work. With a kind yet firm tone, he wanted to ensure I understood the potential difficulties of that career path—emphasizing that social work is not only a challenging profession, but one that is not highly compensated financially. Despite his concerns, he assured me that no matter what I chose, he had my back and would support me however I needed. True to his word, over my seventeen-year social work career, both my father and mother have been encouraging presences.

After completing my Bachelor of Social Work, I immediately began my career at Berks County Children and Youth. Despite the job not being well-regarded due to misconceptions about taking children away from their homes, I was determined to make a positive impact on the lives of vulnerable children. I conducted investigations of suspected child abuse and was also part of a team that attended child death autopsies. These experiences exposed me to the worst of humanity, but they also reinforced my determination to help those in need.

One particular incident during an autopsy of a baby who died from shaken baby syndrome became a turning point in my career. Witnessing the examination of the body and then going home to hold my own child made me realize that I have seen the worst that I possibly could and could not continue in the field of child abuse investigations. That experience while I was attending the University of Pennsylvania pursuing my master's degree taught me that sometimes, it is important to recognize when a job or career is not the right fit for you. It is okay to move on and find something that aligns better with your values and personal well-being. It is also important to prioritize self-care and make decisions that are best for your mental and emotional health.

After eight years as a child abuse investigator, I decided it was time for a change. I applied for a Program Manager position at Berks County Mental Health and Developmental Disabilities Program. This was a grant-funded role working with sixteen to twenty-five-year-olds who had mental health diagnoses or were at risk for developing one. It was a million-dollar grant, and I felt blessed to have the opportunity to raise awareness and provide education to our community about mental health and suicide prevention.

I was in this position for two years when my career took another unexpected turn. The principal of Reading High School contacted me, asking if I would be interested in becoming their school social worker. Intrigued by the potential, I went for an interview and was immediately drawn in by the students and community. Though different from my county mental health work, I decided to take a chance on this refreshing change of pace. I told my boss at Berks County Mental Health and Developmental Disabilities Program, "There are two years left of this grant, and I want to see this through." They kept me on part-time so that I could finish the grant. We did some cool things together, so my Reading High School work coexisted with the county grant position.

Though I loved my job at Reading and never imagined leaving, an unexpected opportunity arose. One day, a neighboring school district announced they were establishing a new social work program at Muhlenberg School District. Their superintendent had a strong belief in the importance of mental health support and recognized the value social workers could provide. Intrigued, I went to the interview and immediately felt a sense of belonging. To my surprise, the superintendent not only offered me the social worker position but asked me to take on an administrative role overseeing the development of the new program.

As Muhlenberg School District's first-ever social worker hire, there were some initial growing pains as we worked to define the distinct roles of school counselors versus social workers. But we collaborated to establish our niches, and the program has flourished. Today, we have a team of four social workers, one in each of the district's four school buildings.

My duties include conducting suicide risk assessments, performing mental health check-ins for high school students, and supporting students with IEPs. We also connect families with any outside resources they may need. One aspect I love about this job is how we remove barriers for students to access therapy and counseling services right at school. Students can simply get the help they need during a study hall period. It's truly a one-stop shop for mental health care right in the school building.

One of the highlights and most memorable achievements of my career was starting the Aevidum student mental health club at Reading High School. Aevidum, meaning "I've got your back" in Latin, began at a high school in Lancaster County after a devastating student suicide. In the aftermath, a teacher gathered students to process what happened. Symbolically, there was an empty chair for the student who had died. Sitting together, the students started an organic dialogue, asking poignant questions like, "Why aren't we openly talking about mental health? What should we do with this chair?"

From that raw conversation emerged Aevidum, a movement to destigmatize mental illness and create spaces for vulnerable youth to support each other. Soon, similar student-led Aevidum chapters began sprouting up in schools across Pennsylvania.

When I started at Reading High on day one, I brought this powerful idea to the principal, proposing we launch our own Aevidum club. He was skeptical, admitting, "Social work is new here. Openly talking about mental health is new. I really don't know if you're going to be successful bringing a club like that into our building, but I will support whatever it is you want to do." I was determined to plant those seeds, undeterred. I started small—putting up flyers, making morning announcements, and intentionally meeting as many students as I could face-to-face. The interest quickly snowballed. Over 80 students attended that very first introductory meeting! It was clear this was filling a gaping need.

As an empathetic, passionate person, I was so emotionally overwhelmed seeing that packed room. Tears started streaming down my face. "This isn't field hockey sign-ups," I managed through the tears. "This is a mental health club." The students looked back simply and matter-of-factly: "Yeah, we know. We're here for it. Let's go!" It was surreal, like a dream. But also, so beautifully real, raw, and exactly what those kids were craving. In that moment, I knew without a doubt that I had found my true calling.

Self-Care Tips

Self-care is an utmost priority for me, both as a human being and especially as a social worker. I make time for practices that nourish my mind and body, like yoga and meditation. I value spending time in nature and find joy in simple pleasures like reading and traveling. Having a supportive husband and close-knit group of friends helps me maintain a healthy work-life balance. Above all, I cherish quality time spent with my two sons, who light up my world.

The importance of self-care and open communication are core values I strive to embody daily. I intentionally engage in activities I genuinely enjoy that make me feel good. If I'm feeling overwhelmed, I'm not afraid to step back and take a break—including using a mental health day when needed. Replenishing myself allows me to show up more fully as a present parent, partner, friend, and social worker. Remember, putting on your own oxygen mask first allows you to be of maximum service to others over the long run. Build the habits of taking care of yourself now, and you'll be able to make this career sustainable and rewarding for years to come.

Practice Wisdom and Advice

- Drawing from my own experiences and growth over the years as a social worker, my most valuable advice is to prioritize self-care above all else. Taking care of oneself—mind, body, and spirit—is essential to effectively care for others. This includes setting firm boundaries around your time and capacity, learning to say no when needed, and not overextending yourself. It also means building in non-negotiable practices for your own well-being like exercise, meditation, reading, or simply unplugging from work.

- Seeking support is vital—both personally and professionally. Cultivating a strong network of friends, loved ones, and colleagues you can lean on prevents isolation and burnout. Make time for meaningful social connection outside of work. At the office, find coworkers you click with to grab coffee, vent, or laugh together. Most importantly, find a clinical supervisor who is experienced and empathetic, and can provide the guidance and mentorship you need to develop and maintain health practices.
- Striking a sustainable balance between your personal life and the intensity of this work is an ongoing process. Consciously set limits around working hours, make your personal time protected, and don't allow work to constantly bleed into home life. Have interests and hobbies separate from your job to immerse yourself in. Take your paid time off. When you prioritize your own needs, you'll show up more fully present and engaged for the important work.

Final Thoughts

In my view, the pervasive stigma surrounding mental health issues and seeking treatment remains one of the biggest obstacles facing the social work profession. While progress has certainly been made in recent years to open more mainstream conversations and reduce some of the shame, there is still a tremendous amount of work ahead to fully normalize and destigmatize mental illness in our society. Too often, mental health conditions are still seen as signs of weakness, unworthiness, or defects, rather than real medical issues deserving of care, empathy, and support. Shifting these deeply ingrained societal attitudes is an enormous challenge. The general lack of resources within the mental health field also poses significant hurdles.

From my firsthand experiences working with clients over the years, I've observed that the biggest overarching challenge they face is a severe lack of resources and support systems.

Many of the individuals I've served simply do not have a strong network of family, friends, or community to lean on during difficult times. The dearth of genuinely affordable treatment options and services for those without insurance or financial means further compounds these challenges. Even just finding a therapist taking new patients on a sliding scale in their community proves a lofty barrier for most. Navigating complex systems to get connected with the few available resources that may exist adds another layer of stress and bureaucracy. Strengthening human services and making it widely available is crucial to empowering progress for all.

In Conclusion: Passion + Purpose = Social Work

I feel like social work is in my blood—an intrinsic part of my identity. I believe fundamentally that every human being deserves to feel loved, feel seen, and be given chances, despite this often cruel world where we have no idea what silent struggles others are facing. My role is to listen without judgment, let people's truths be spoken, and hold an empowering belief that positive change is possible for everyone. Building meaningful relationships and connections is hands-down my favorite part of this job and the heart of social work.

From earliest visions of teaching young children to the intense experiences in child welfare, to this school-based community role, my story is indeed one of following an evolving passion toward the purpose of making a real difference in the lives of vulnerable individuals. The journey of a social worker is often filled with challenges, but it is also incredibly rewarding.

In sharing my social work story, my hope is that you can feel my passion, resilience, and dedication required to make a positive impact on the lives of vulnerable individuals. By recognizing the need for change, embracing new opportunities, and prioritizing self-care, I have found fulfillment in my role as a social worker. I continue to hope that through my work, I have left a lasting impact on the lives of those I have served, and my commitment to advocating for mental health continues to make a difference. The world will always need more trailblazers committed to making a real, lasting difference in the lives of those rendered most vulnerable.

Using Advocacy and Passion to Create Change

Maegan Llerena, LSW
MSW: Temple University
BSW: Cedar Crest College

Social Work Pathway and Work Experience

Maegan Llerena, LSW

My parents came to the United States from Peru to have a better life, leaving a lot of family behind. We started out in Harlem, New York, and my parents decided we should move to Pennsylvania to give me and my brother an even better life, and we ended up in Bethlehem.

Being the oldest daughter, I took on a lot of responsibility whether I wanted to or not. Although generally I was a very good student, I wound up getting expelled, so my education was a little sloppy. I recognized I always felt very connected to young folks, and because of graduation requirements by the school district, I completed my community service at an elementary school. I always loved working with kids, perhaps because I feel like I missed out on a lot of my childhood. Also, I wanted to make sure they had opportunities that I did not and make them aware of pathways they did not know were possible.

I went to Northampton Community College (NCC) in Bethlehem, which felt like the right place to start my path so I could gain some base knowledge I missed out on in high school. I thought I had to major in criminal justice to work with kids who needed support, but I never felt the connection nor passion for the major.

When I took an Introduction to Social Work course, I realized that was what I was passionate about. I became the President of the Social Work Club and participated on a service trip to Ecuador. My favorite memories are from my time at NCC. I transferred to the social work BSW program at Cedar Crest College, getting a grounding in the knowledge, values, and skills needed to be a social worker.

After graduation, I took some time off from school and worked at Valley Youth House in Bethlehem, Pennsylvania, for a year. I felt very connected to the kids. Two things that really kept sticking out to me were that trauma is hard and most of my clients were Latino or Black.

I worked with families that dealt with intense trauma. What was interesting to me was many families wanted the child or adolescent to "just get over" the trauma and move on. I quickly realized that micro work was not the path for me. I thought, *If we fix the world, kids wouldn't have to go through this.*

Because I had just received my BSW, I had to be partnered with an MSW. My partner was white. Clients would say, "It's so good to have you because you speak our language," or "You look like us," or "You understand what we're saying." Some moments, I could vividly see the disconnect between my partner with the MSW and our clients, who were primarily Black and/or Latino. For example, she didn't understand some common phrases that Latinos use. I saw how crucial it was for me to do this work as a brown woman, and at the same time I kept thinking, *The world is so messed up. I want to do something that will impact multiple people at a time, something that is bigger.*

I decided to go back to graduate school. I went for an interview for my internship. I remember walking into the first office of Make the Road Pennsylvania in the city of Reading.

They were trying to expand to Allentown at the time, which is where I live. When I tried to set up my interview, they thought I was white based on my maiden name. Because the organization is focused on immigrant rights for Latinx folks, my predecessor told me he wondered, "Who's this white girl trying to work with immigrants in Pennsylvania?" There was so much chaos in the background of the phone call, I could barely hear the person I was trying to set up an interview with.

In that moment, I knew that's what I wanted to do, and I didn't even have the interview yet! I went for the interview in a tiny office with handmade signs. It was very grassroots organizing. I was like, *I love it. I'm in love.*

My predecessor said, "I'm not trying to convince you that you should switch from clinical to macro."

I replied, "I'm convinced." They asked me to open the Allentown office for Make the Road PA and I have been there almost seven years now! I started as an Intern, became the Program Director, then the Deputy Director. I became the Executive Director in 2019 at the age of twenty-five.

Make the Road PA primarily focuses on social, racial, and economic justice issues. We also do civic engagement work, advocacy, and education. We help people register to vote and educate them on how voting works and when elections are coming up. The issues we work on are decided by community members who are best equipped to speak on their lived experiences. They get to decide the work that we do, the tactics we will take, and the stories we tell based on their communities, their backgrounds, and the campaigns we work on. Our work is dependent on what the community members say is a problem. We work on solutions.

I did not finish my MSW at the original school I attended. Instead, I completed my MSW at Temple University in Philadelphia, Pennsylvania, as an advanced standing student with a focus on macro social work. It was important for my own personal growth to go to a school that had a macro track for social work. My MSW internship was with an organization where I helped conduct research on the poorest zip codes in Philadelphia and how the uprisings and increasing gun violence are impacting youth in those zip codes. I had to redistribute my workload to complete my MSW, which required bringing in my colleagues at Make the Road PA to take on some responsibilities. Since then, rather than take back those responsibilities, I began to take on more work building the infrastructure of our national organization. It was always interesting to me the lack of Latinas in social work. There was only one in one of my classes, a clinical course, and I have never had a professor whom I could identify with. This is pushing me to potentially go back to school for a DSW to be able to teach in my field.

Self-Care Tips

I am a hard-core gym girl! The gym has become my own spiritual practice. When I first took the job, I was so stressed from the chaos that came with the weight of the role that I did not realize how much I stopped caring for myself. It was deeply impacting my overall health and my body. I gained weight, and then gained more weight, and I felt so unhealthy. My job took over my life.

In 2020, right before the pandemic I thought, *This is my chance*. I started working out. I have never looked back, and the gym is my favorite place to go. I go every day and on the weekends. I also go at a time that's ridiculously early so I do not have to answer the phone, and no one would bother me anyway because it is so early! That's been my salvation, and it makes me feel very good about myself.

Practice Wisdom and Advice

• Realize networking is your friend. You can learn about opportunities you would never have thought of. You don't have to become best friends with everyone nor stay in touch with them on a regular basis—just see what opportunities arise. Get to know social workers and folks who are not social workers.

- Talk about things other than your job. Having other types of conversations is important. It gives you the ability to step away from your work.
- Don't be afraid to try something new. Just because it doesn't seem like it is related to your field, but you are interested in it, try it. Stepping out of your comfort zones will help you figure out what you do and do not like. Consider doing some volunteer work to see if that's something you really want to do.
- Find a therapist. Some people go into social work because they have gone through some challenging life situations, and I think it's important to find yourself a therapist to figure out your triggers, so they do not come out in your work.

Final Thoughts

What has been most challenging for me is switching from using anger as a motivator to create change to operating from a place of love.

Also, I don't believe in one person making all the decisions. We use a team approach to decision-making. I wanted to make sure that I'm leading with a mindset of abundance. It is hard sometimes because there are so many things happening in the world that force you to make quick decisions, but the reality of it is, some decisions deserve more intentional processing before making a final decision. I oversee thirty people, and my worst fear is having to lay off someone, so juggling finances and other administrative responsibilities is challenging as well.

What truly has been a highlight of my career so far is my organizing work around issues that I care deeply about. I am also very proud of how the organization has grown in the past seven years. When I became the Executive Director, we had a staff of seven, and now we have a staff of thirty with a multi-million-dollar budget! It's exciting to create healthy careers for folks where they stay for a long time and grow as individuals and professionally. I am passionate about macro social work and creating change in systems and policies.

My Passion for Clinical Work

Abby Feinberg, LCSW
MSW: Smith College
BA: University of Connecticut

Social Work Pathway and Work Experience

My pathway to social work was interesting because I originally wanted to be in elementary education. As an undergraduate, I was very involved with kids and teaching as much as possible in elementary schools in Pennsylvania, the state I am from, and in Connecticut, where I went to college. The feedback I received was I would have been a fantastic teacher thirty years ago, but today's expectations for teachers are rigid and structured. When

Abby Feinberg, LCSW

I created a lesson plan, everyone loved it, and other classes wanted to use it. But I was told that I would not have been able to use this lesson plan as a teacher in the school because I had combined different parts of the curriculum, which had to be taught in order.

At the University of Connecticut, I originally pursued a dual degree in elementary education and English. When I felt too restricted by elementary education, I thought, *I'll pursue becoming an English professor, to have more flexibility and leeway*. When I was halfway through my junior year, I realized that the Psychology 101 general education course I had taken freshman year was the perfect fit. I reached out to the professor, who became an ongoing mentor for me. I finished my psychology degree in the last three semesters as an undergraduate along with my English degree.

When I graduated, I worked for two years as a mental health worker at a partial hospital program. It was an intensive day program that bridged the gap between hospitalization and outpatient for mental health. Because my coworkers knew I was interested in becoming a therapist, I was allowed to sit in on some clinical group therapy sessions. I consulted with different people about whether I wanted to pursue psychology or social work. Through my work, I met someone who had gone to Smith College in Northampton, Massachusetts, for social work, a clinical focused program, which was a perfect fit for me. I also liked how the program was structured. I was happy to be accepted there because I was interested in learning various therapeutic interventions and loved the microwork, the one-on-one therapy. I really wanted the social work degree because of the person-in-environment perspective. People are not just how they present in the office. They play different roles in their lives, and they're affected by all the components of their past and present and society. By the time I graduated from Smith, I felt well prepared between the academic learning and my internships.

After I graduated from Smith, my husband and I moved back to Pennsylvania. During one summer break from college, I had worked at KidsPeace in Orefield, Pennsylvania, as a Mental Health Worker, and a summer Unit Aide in the residential program. After returning to Pennsylvania and obtaining my MSW, I was offered a position at KidsPeace in their hospital program. Although I had wanted to do outpatient work, I decided to take the job because it was salary rather than fee for service. I learned a lot and obtained the supervision I needed toward my LCSW. I highly recommend even the shortest amount of time working in a psychiatric hospital at the start of a social work career.

The job got tough. I also learned that unlike some of my coworkers, I was not passionate about the quick client turnaround, and the focus on crisis management. I always wanted to delve deeper with my clients, but that was not how the hospital worked. One of my supervisors said, "I think you would really like the residential program."

After about a year and a half at the hospital, I switched to the residential program, and she was right. I absolutely loved it. I got to continue enjoying the collaborative effort of a multidisciplinary team, with the additional opportunity to clinically engage with adolescents and families through their concerns. Each day, I went to work knowing I had supportive coworkers whom I could bounce ideas off, brainstorm with, and learn from. I realized how different it would have been in an outpatient setting, where it's possible, and often likely, that the only interactions are with clients, rather than with coworkers. The average length of stay was about four to six months. Even "short-term" clients stayed for six weeks, which was longer than the seven to ten days in the hospital. I could get into more therapeutic interventions I enjoyed. I really thrived there and loved what I was doing.

As it parallels teaching, and can be individually catered, I was always interested in providing supervision. I was approved by an intern's master's program to provide supervision, before being eligible to do so on my own. I took it seriously as a supervisee as well. In addition to receiving supervision at KidsPeace, I sought out, and paid for, additional clinical supervision. I wanted to make sure I was getting clinical supervision consistently. Supervision at work can be interrupted based on scheduling and company prioritizing, and it often has a focus on administrative tasks. After earning my LCSW, I became a Senior Clinician at KidsPeace and provided individual and group supervision for those working toward their license.

Then I was sought out by a company called Senior Care Therapy, which focuses on geriatric work. The idea of working with the geriatric population was very intriguing to me because I had already had so much experience with children, adolescents, and families. I am always up for learning and exploring, and I was drawn to the residential agency. I would be working with a multidisciplinary team, and I would grow by learning about death, dying, and life review. Those topics scared me, and I wanted to better understand them.

Working with people at the end of their lives was special. What I realized is people at this stage are not necessarily seeking therapy. I learned to work differently with the patients because they especially valued being heard and respected. One aspect that was very similar between the adolescent and the geriatric populations, especially within a residential setting, was the theme of longing for more autonomy and control over their lives, and feeling restricted, trapped, and helpless. Working with people at the end of their lives, helping them make meaning out of their lives, was very special. However, the acuity level was a significant shift for me. I realized what therapy looked like in this setting and had to adjust. I enjoyed the job, but I was aware of not experiencing the same level of passion I had for deeper clinical work.

I went on maternity leave and was sought out by the company I currently work for, Thriveworks Counseling, doing outpatient therapy in person and online. I love it. I always wanted to do outpatient therapy, and through this long process of learning, growing, experimenting, and challenging myself, I'm finally doing outpatient therapy with adults! I identify as an integrative clinician and use various modalities because I really commit to the client. I'm willing to be flexible and use whatever is going to work for them. I continue to learn new therapeutic modalities. Most recently I have been trained in using Eye Movement Desensitization and Reprocessing (EMDR).

A highlight of my career was a client I had at KidsPeace. The client's parents were high-ranking in the military. When I spoke with them on the phone, I recommended what could be helpful during an upcoming home pass. The parents pretty much said to me, "You don't know anything, you little girl. That won't work in our family. That's not how we do things." It was challenging for me to have a courageous conversation, but I said back to them, "You are the expert of your home. I respect that. You know what you can do, what you cannot do, and if that's the way it is, we need to shift our focus. We have to update our expectations for your child because we are lowering the ceiling for what your child is capable of. What we don't want to do is have unrealistic expectations and have the child continually not meet the expectations and feel a sense of failure and disappointment."

It was an uncomfortable phone call, but the next day the parents called and said, "We thought about what you said, and we're able to do what you were recommending."

Termination is super important in therapy, and I like to carve out time for purposeful reflection, encouragement, and discussion. I find it is a healing experience for the client. I ask each client the following five questions, then I answer them myself.

1. What is one thing you learned from or about me?
2. What is one thing you will miss about me?
3. What is one thing you've improved on?
4. What is one thing for you to keep working on?
5. What is one thing you wish for your future?

I also asked the questions to the parents in a back-and-forth format. Then, I would ask the parents and the client to respond to the questions going back and forth with each other because they were ending the relationship they had with the client while in the residential facility. As they reflected on that chapter in their lives, knowing what could go better, what they wish for the future, and what they would miss were always challenging questions.

When I was terminating with this client and their family, they said, "We came into therapy thinking our kid had a problem. We're leaving therapy knowing that our *family* had a problem." The parents shifted to an openness and willingness to see the issue as a family problem. It gave me such goosebumps because I knew my work was done.

Self-Care Tips

I like to practice what I preach. I do my own EMDR and find it very healing when I'm practicing and using coping and regulation skills with my clients. That also helps me throughout the day. I tell my clients that the more you practice it, the more easily accessible it is to you when you need it, and that's been the truth for me as well.

I use deep breathing and listen to saxophone music, which is soothing to me. I like the pitch of the instrument, and hearing it helps me chill.

Even when you don't think you have time for self-care, you can weave in ways of regulating yourself, checking in with yourself, and prioritizing yourself. In graduate school, as a class representative, I advocated that if we took six classes instead of five, we would make it work and adjust accordingly. Given that knowledge, imagine yourself with six classes, with the sixth class for self-care. This puts you in a proactive place to prevent burnout. From day one of graduate school, incorporate self-care into your life and practice what you preach to clients.

Practice Wisdom and Advice

- Explore. If you're new to social work and you have the time and space, explore options whether they're modalities, levels of care, different populations, or jobs. If you're interested in outpatient work and go right into it, you might miss opportunities that you are unlikely to go back and try. Outpatient work is always available to you, so look for other experiences first. Explore to find out what's a good fit for you.
- Seek help. In addition to self-awareness, getting consultation and supervision is important. Go for your own therapy and be transparent and vulnerable in your sessions.
- Set boundaries. I am very conscious of what I share about myself. It varies per setting and per client. One way I have navigated boundaries is by sharing a personal experience, but through the verbiage of "I had a client/friend who … and they said it felt like … ." I found this helped achieve the goals of attunement and validation without shifting the focus to myself, or potentially impacting the therapeutic rapport. At the end of the day, it is always what you think is in your client's best interest.

Final Thoughts

Be self-reflective because we can cause harm to our clients. If you have a reaction to something that your client says to you, that moment of self-knowledge can determine whether or not you are a helpful therapist. If the reaction that you have in yourself is your own stuff and you're not aware of your own stuff, it can get intertwined in the feedback that you give to your client.

Burnout is real. I feel that one of the coolest parts about having an LCSW is you can always bounce to another setting or population so you will not burn out! There are so many opportunities!

Setting Boundaries, Showing Empathy, and Trusting Your Skills

Noelle Serafin, LSW

MSW: Walden University

BSW: Cedar Crest College

Social Work Pathway and Work Experience

Something that motivated me to become a social worker was taking a service trip in 2009 through Northampton Community College in Pennsylvania. We went to New Orleans to help rebuild homes devastated by Hurricane Katrina. The trip really opened my eyes to a whole different world. It felt good to help so many people doing this service work. I also loved the study of people. I thought I wanted to go to school for psychology, and I realized that wasn't exactly what I wanted to do. I didn't even know

Noelle Serafin, LSW

social work existed until I took the Introduction to Social Work course at Northampton Community College. I was sold on social work! I went to Cedar Crest College for my BSW and Walden University for my MSW.

My internships were a big part of the beginning of my social work career. My undergrad placement was at PA Treatment and Healing (PATH), which is a facility for adolescents with a variety of issues. For example, there were juvenile sex offenders and children in foster care with special needs. This was a very intense environment, and I learned quickly how to protect myself as a social worker because the clients didn't care to save or lose anything.

My MSW internship was at the Veterans Administration (VA) Hospital, which was incredible. I had an amazing supervisor who helped me process everything. I didn't realize how important supervision was until I was wrapping up my time at my internship. It's like you're able to unpack your bags and let someone else look through them. Then you think, *All right, I'll bring these to work tomorrow. I am not going to bring it home.* I worked in many different departments at the VA. The veterans also helped me to become a better social worker. They would say to me, "No, that's not a good question to ask. Ask this one."

I worked with intensive mental health cases, which was very eye-opening. This experience really made me love mental health so much because it's like a superpower that people can live with various mental illnesses and still function.

One of my favorite things happened when I was wrapping up my internship at the VA. One of the veterans brought in a guitar. He played and another girl sang the most beautiful song to me as a tribute before I left. They were crying, and they said, "You don't know how much you've impacted our lives." It was very emotional and reaffirming that I chose the right career.

I worked for a school as a Therapeutic Support Staff (TSS) worker, which was fun, but one year of that type of work was enough for me. I worked in home health and hospice, which captured my whole heart. I loved hospice so much because I loved being there for people, especially in the transition of life to death. Being welcomed into people's homes was just such a beautiful thing. Counseling the families was amazing too.

I did outpatient therapy for middle school, and I'm currently a school social worker. Being a school social worker is like organized chaos. I have individual and group sessions. I work in the school district with first through twelfth graders and also with college students at a local community college. What is most challenging is setting and maintaining firm boundaries and not letting my heart leave my professional self. You want to give so much of yourself, and you want to be available. But you can't be available at two in the morning because that blurs the boundaries. You must be strong about the fact that you're not going to adopt the kids who need to be adopted, something difficult for me, because you see that they would do so well with just a little bit more love.

An experience on my social work journey that stands out to me was that one day, I did not feel well and thought about not going to work. I thought, *Let me go in. For some reason I feel like I must be there.* I called one of my students down, and we couldn't find her. I was looking all over the school and thought, *Maybe some kind of teenage crisis is going on* so we checked the bathrooms. She came out of the bathroom with a note in her hand. She handed it to me and said, "I took a bunch of pills this morning." I didn't know what kind and I was worried. We went into my office before I was going to make the report, and I tried to get information out of her. She said, "If you weren't here," and she threw out a bunch of pills, "I was going to take the rest of these." This situation continues to stand out to me since I was the only person in the world she felt wanted her here. I make it very clear ever since that day that I'm not the only one. There are other people, but most importantly, it's you yourself that's going to save yourself. We had a rocky relationship, and I was always very honest with her. She said I was the only person who was ever confrontational with her, and she needed that in her life. So thankfully, she was okay. She went and got treatment. I was the one who made the horrible phone call to her mom, and I cried with her mom because it was an emotional time. I think showing emotion as a social worker is important, not all the time, but for certain reasons. That was a big moment for me, realizing the impact of my work.

Self-Care Tips

When I started in social work, I noticed that some social workers did not take care of themselves. They just took care of other people. I thought about leaving the field worried I might be that way and be unhappy. We must take care of ourselves and put ourselves first. Self-care is important.

I love spending time with my family, especially uninterrupted fun time during the holidays. I love cooking and baking. I take trips with my girlfriends such as to the wine country. I like to go on hikes with my friends. I value anything that helps me to enjoy the moment and be present in it.

Time in nature is healing for Noelle Serafin, LSW.

Practice Wisdom and Advice

- Remember that you're not always prepared for the things you're going to see. You're just not. And that's okay. I think of myself like a duck on the water, with the feet constantly flapping. Underlying, I know I have developed the skills and knowledge from my education.
- Consider trying an element of social work you don't think you'll like. I didn't think I'd like hospice at all, but it turned out to be such a beautiful experience. It's important to try all the different practice areas to find your niche.
- Find mentors. My most favorite mentor is the author of this book, Hope Horowitz, who has always given me such great advice and who saw so much in me before I could see it in myself. Going with Hope on the first trip to New Orleans was the best thing that ever happened to me. She taught me how to meditate when we were there, and it was exactly what I needed at the exact right time.
- Keep in touch with your emotions. My wonderful professors at Cedar Crest College made it a point to show that they

were very hard lined and did not show emotion. I was going through a divorce when I got my bachelor's degree and let all my professors know, and I cried. In a very professional manner, one professor said, "Everything is fine. You will get through this." A few weeks later right before graduation, I received a prestigious social work award. It was awarded to only one person graduating from social work that year. My professor took me into the office and was emotional saying to me, "You thrived in this whole situation, and I am so proud of you." Those words and emotion meant so much to me at that time. It showed me there are times it is okay to be emotional as we are human as well. This proved helpful to prepare me to deal with crises that happen in the field.

Final Thoughts

The one skill I learned that has helped me all around is confrontation and being honest when I'm uncomfortable. When I don't like something or when somebody says something that makes me feel uncomfortable, I have no problem saying, "I don't like that. Could you change the way you worded that?" Before becoming a social worker, I would just let anybody say whatever they wanted to me. I realize that I'm not helping my clients by letting them talk to or treat people disrespectfully. Once I realized in my personal life I wasn't holding the same values to myself that I hold to my clients, I began using this skill in my personal life as well.

My social work career has shaped me to be the best version of myself. I take a second to think about my reactions to people, so I am not judgmental. I keep myself in a positive bubble in my mind because I know that the alternative is being unhappy. I constantly utilize my own coping skills that I'm sharing with my clients. It has made me a much better mother because I'm present all the time.

Resilience, Persistence, and Seizing Opportunities

Viviana Lucabeche, PhD, LCSW
PhD: Widener University
MSW: University of Pennsylvania
BA: Social Work, Muhlenberg College

Social Work Pathway and Work Experience

I grew up in Chile under a military government that most would consider oppressive. Since I was very young, I do not remember much, although my family left shortly before the military coupe of 1973 took place. We did return to Chile after a tumultuous time in the United States.

Viviana Lucabeche, PhD, LCSW

My mother told me that my dad came to the United States first, and my mother, sister, and I followed a year later, traveling through Mexico and staying there for a couple of months. My mother told me that we went through customs and crossed the border in the back of a car with blankets covering us.

When we arrived in the United States, I did not speak English. In grade school, they pulled me out of class to take ESL classes. I felt the other kids didn't want to be around me and often made fun of me because I did not speak the language, so I didn't have any friends.

We were poor, my parents could not find steady work, and we were dealing with immigration. We were the vulnerable population. I learned early on not to get attached to anything because we often had to move quickly, leaving everything behind. I felt very alone and alienated. We kept getting denied visas that would allow us to stay legally and change our undocumented status. After numerous denied petitions, my parents decided to move back to Chile.

After we moved back to Chile, even though it was a tumultuous time, I preferred my life there. I spoke the language, had friends, and lived in a neighborhood with a strong sense of community. It didn't feel as oppressive as it did in the United States, because in the United States poverty had a different meaning. In Chile, we had community, so there were interpersonal connections despite what was going on politically. In Chile, I felt as though I belonged.

Due to the dictatorship, it became a natural part of life to see military personnel with guns, and I remember the fear that went with that. The Chilean people are resilient, and I recall seeing people passionately protesting and demonstrating because they felt the government was robbing them of their culture and freedom. One time I got caught in a protest where tear gas was dispersed, and I can still remember that horrible feeling of struggling to breathe. People were protesting government they believed was oppressive. Augusto Pinochet, the President, was a self-proclaimed magnanimous leader who wanted to be loved; however, he liked order, so we had to follow curfews. People who did not follow the curfews or talked against the government were beaten and/or arrested. Hearing gun shots and bombings was a normal part of my life at the time. Growing up under this rule affected me so much that to this day I still jump at loud, sudden noises.

I came back to the United States to get married and became a citizen under a fiancée visa. I had my son, and eventually the marriage did not work out. I found myself single with a child and limited employment options. Although I had done a good deal of work in human services in the Hispanic community because I was bilingual, without a degree my options were limited. At that point, knowing I was responsible for my son's well-being, I had to find a way to get a degree to secure a future for both of us.

I walked into Muhlenberg College because I was passed over for a promotion since I did not have a degree. One of the admissions counselors said, "If you start today and enroll in one course this semester, we will pay for a second course." Up until this point, I really struggled with my college trajectory. I was in and out of school because I faced many barriers. Money was a struggle, plus I needed to balance my role as a mother, student, and full-time worker.

At Muhlenberg College, I was one of the first five recipients of a Latino merit scholarship. The year I applied for the scholarship, Muhlenberg received more than two hundred applicants. I figured that if Muhlenberg was going to invest money in me, I had to stick it through even if I could take only two classes each semester. I was determined to finish. I saw my scholarship as the great equalizer. It was also important for me to be a role model to my family.

I thought I would major in psychology because I wanted to help people and had experience working in human services. By my third psychology course, I realized it was not for me. I thought, *This is not about helping people.* I went to the dean for guidance.

"Tell me what you want to do," she said.

"I want to work with people and help them in a meaningful way," I said.

"It sounds like social work is the career for you," she said.

Once I found social work, I never looked back. Muhlenberg did not offer a BSW as a major, so they worked with me to earn a BA in social work.

I started to see how my experiences as a member of a vulnerable population were significant in my chosen profession. I recalled my outcry for social justice even as a child, I could not accept it was the norm to not let me speak because I was a girl. I could not accept that I couldn't voice my opinions just because the government said I couldn't do it. Social work was a natural fit for me since I was learning to be an advocate.

In my last year at Muhlenberg College, my mentor, who had been instrumental in helping me get my scholarship and on my career path, Sam Laposata, asked me if I wanted to apply to the University of Pennsylvania for an MSW. He said Muhlenberg College would sponsor my first year. By this time, I had another son, and I understood that an education would ensure our future. That opportunity helped me gain my MSW, and then I went on to earn my PhD from Widener University.

I have had many experiences as a social worker, including working with clients with substance use disorders, mental health issues, eating disorders, trauma, and anger management. I have worked mainly with adults, but with different populations, including the homeless, minorities, and LGBTQ populations.

I've worked in hospitals and even as a professor in a seminary. I was also the only social worker in a college's Department of Counseling Psychology. Now, I'm a professor teaching BSW and MSW students at Bloomsburg University of Pennsylvania.

One highlight of my practice as a clinical social worker was when a client experienced an "aha" moment. He was a veteran suffering from PTSD. He could not access his VA benefits soon enough for counseling care. There was a six-month waitlist at the time, and he could not wait that long. I can't even remember how many weeks into the therapeutic process we were when he had the "aha" moment where things clicked for him, and his healing began. To me, that is the most rewarding part of being a clinician. It does not happen all the time, so when it does, it is very rewarding to know you have helped someone.

I think one of the most challenging issues I encountered is access to resources. What we teach in social work school might not always be the reality in practice when we try to connect clients with the services they need. There are many hoops to jump through, and some populations are so disadvantaged that they might never access the actual services or medications they need. Even when I did private practice and people were paying, we were frustrated by the limited mental health and drug and alcohol services available for people in general.

Self-Care Tips

Self-care is a daily, ongoing process. It is not about taking a monthly trip. It must be part of your routine like eating or drinking water. If I had known this early in my career, I probably could have avoided the burnout that I experienced.

Don't be afraid to ask for help. We are in a helping profession, but we don't ask one another for help. How are we going to do this alone? Find somebody whom you can trust to ask for help. You don't have all the answers. Eventually you might learn a lot more by asking for help. I also talk to my husband to express my emotions.

Don't be afraid to change. One of the fascinating things about being a social worker is the diversity of things you can do with this degree. If you don't like what you're doing, don't leave the profession. Find something else that you love.

I have learned to shut things off. I believe it is important to turn off your phone and shut your brain down for five to ten minutes a day. I do this daily.

I exercise. I don't love exercising, but I do it because I know it is healthy.

I love to read good books that have nothing to do with social work. Books like thrillers and historical fiction provide a great escape.

Practice Wisdom and Advice

- Remember social work's six core values. By the time we start to practice, we have internalized them without even realizing it. In a few years, you realize how these values have been integrated into your life. The core values have shaped me as a person, and they have been essential for my professional growth and development.
- Keep in mind everyone deserves a second chance because everyone is capable of change. That guides my work and aligns with social work's core values and mission. I've faced so many challenges. I've been knocked down so many times, yet I have been able to stand back up. I learned to ask for help. And because I know what it feels like to have to ask for help, I can appreciate that from my clients. My philosophy is to never forget where you came from.
- Have supervision. It is essential. I think if we had better supervision, we would see fewer ethical violations. I think

that there are two types of supervision: administrative supervision and clinical supervision. I've had a lot of experience as a clinical supervisor, which is very different than administrative. When I was working to get my LCSW (we must get three years post-master's clinical supervision), the agency I was working at didn't have an MSW, let alone an LCSW, so they hired someone to supervise me. Because she was not a part of the agency, her supervision made me a better social worker and a better person.

The supervision process is the parallel process between a social worker and client to feel they are in a safe place to process any issues that might be surfacing from their sessions, such as self-doubt or anything that relates to their ability to communicate and to provide effective services with their clients.

Social work tends to have limited resources, so supervisors don't always have time to provide that type of clinical supervision. They only have time to sign off on charts and worry about the administrative items, and not necessarily about the growth and development of a social worker.

Final Thoughts

I would like us as a profession to take better care of our professional identity and one another. Our profession was founded to help the disadvantaged and poor. But I think somewhere along the way we forgot about nurturing ourselves.

Also, we have worked hard to gain credibility for this degree. Yet still people have trouble conceptualizing what it means to teach social work, let alone earn a PhD in Social Work and what that means. We need to do better in promoting our professional identity because it affects the people we serve. We need to put more attention and energy into us as a profession.

We will all need help at some point in our lives. I would not be where I am without the support from my family, mentor, and friends. An African proverb that continues to inspire me and, I believe, captures my relationship with my sons and husband is "If you want to go fast, go alone. If you want to go far, go together."

Compassion, Advocacy, and Persistence

Stuart Horowitz, LCSW, ACSW
MSW: Marywood University
BA: Psychology and Sociology: Wayne State University

Social Work Pathway and Work Experience

A combination of my own personal experiences and my interest in mental health and the human condition moved me toward a career in social work. Full disclosure is I wanted to be a therapist, and I started off in psychology. I recognized the graduate program in psychology I was attending was not for me. Through the

Stuart Horowitz, LCSW, Speaking at an NASW Legislative Education and Advocacy Day at the Capitol in Harrisburg, PA

encouragement of my wife, I decided to pursue a social work degree at Marywood University, recognizing a career in social work would lead me to my goal of becoming a psychotherapist. I realized I'm more of an experiential learner, and Marywood gave me the opportunity to not just read, but really put the learning into practice. Social work opened the door to so many other opportunities.

Throughout my thirty-two-year career, I primarily focused on providing outpatient therapy. I also consulted at a nursing home for ten years providing advice on mental health issues. I did on-call crisis intervention work for a hospital. I also worked on two different psychiatric units. One was a general psychiatric unit, and the other focused on psychological trauma. I also did case management on that unit as well as group work.

In the job I retired from at the hospital in 2019, I was an outpatient therapist. As an outpatient therapist, I worked with individuals, couples, and families and treated multiple mental health disorders. I also coordinated the social work student internship program. I always valued supervising students working to get their master's degree in social work. I felt it was important to prepare the next generation of social workers so they understand how to put theory to practice.

I have taught at different educational levels, including community college and social work bachelor's and master's programs. Courses I teach or have taught include sociology, psychology, and various social work courses. Because I am an LCSW (licensed clinical social worker), I have and continue to supervise social workers who are working on their clinical license.

Even in retirement, I remain active contributing to social work causes. I continue to teach sociology courses at the local community college both online and on campus and maintain a small private practice. I am involved with Resilient Lehigh Valley, which seeks to strengthen communities and address mental health concerns, and with Sandy Hook Promise, advocating to stop gun violence. I recently helped write a curriculum for teachers for Sandy Hook Promise on mindfulness and how to become a trusting adult. I continue to serve on some local boards and serve as the chair of the clinical committee for Jewish Family Service of the Lehigh Valley, which advises on mental health issues.

Another important part of social work is being involved in our professional organization, the National Association of Social Workers (NASW). I served for three years as President of the statewide Pennsylvania Chapter and President-Elect for one year. I was also Vice President for two years, and I did some committee work for the local Division. Volunteering was rewarding, and it gave me an opportunity to meet people from diverse social work backgrounds and advocate for our profession. These roles were more administrative, which was in some ways very different for me and provided a great learning opportunity. I live by the quote, "If I'm not for myself, who will be for me, and if I'm only for myself, then who am I for? And if not now, when?" What this means to me is we must have a balance between taking care of our profession and taking care of the populations we serve. As Vice President, I firmly believed that we could do both to take care of our organization and the populations we serve, and the time was now. Further "if not now, when" means getting beyond the discussion and getting into action and intent. This is exemplified by our profession valuing helping people, raising our voices, and advocating.

When I became President of NASW PA, one of my goals was to get the bill passed that would legally permit social workers to diagnose and have practice protection. This was important because any practitioner, even someone who lost their license in another state, could claim to have qualifications to provide social work services in the state without penalty.

In order to get the bill passed, we mobilized and kept calling legislators to vote for the bill. Their response was that they recognized who we were, and this raised our status. Legislators were telling us, "We know who you are," and they wanted us to stop calling! My mottos were "failure was not an option" and "we'll stop calling when you pass this bill." During the first year of my presidency in 2018, the bill finally passed. Only licensed clinical social workers (LCSW) are allowed to provide *clinical* social work services within the state, including being able to legally diagnose. This is now a protected right. I'm very proud that we finally got it done!

Self-Care Tips

As a social worker, we see the dark side of the world. Most people don't see the world that we see. Speaking for myself,

Stuart Horowitz, LCSW

you really get to know people, and you also get to hear their traumas, struggles, and challenges. It can be draining at an emotional, physical, and cognitive level. By the end of the day, I could feel very drained, and it was challenging to not let other people's traumas overtake me.

For self-care, first, I appreciate the support from my family. I could always talk to my wife, and as my kids got older, I could talk to them. They helped me to process my thoughts and feelings.

Other self-care I practice includes twenty to thirty minutes of meditating each day. I became an avid exerciser and try to work out at least three times a week, lifting weights and doing nautilus and aerobics.

I watch what I eat, and that has become more important over time. I also relax by enjoying activities like going to a movie. I took up yoga and became a yoga instructor when I retired and then started studying karate. Toward the end of my career, I tuned into mindfulness. I had already been practicing mindfulness by meditating for close to fifty years.

Practice Wisdom and Advice

- Learn how to take care of yourself. Social work can be rewarding and you can also burn out.
- Learn to recognize when you are burning out. Take breaks.
- Go on vacation.
- Seek support.
- Find activities to reduce stress.
- Set and know your limits and boundaries.
- Pace yourself.

Stuart Horowitz, LCSW, speaking at an NASW continuing education workshop held at Northampton Community College

Final Thoughts

Social work has had a profound impact on my life. Social work teaches about person and environment, and I've learned to look at the environment in its entirety, including looking at myself and being self-aware. This is very much about mindfulness and "conscious use of self." There were times when I looked at myself and could apply it to my clients. For example, I had a personal experience where I recognized that some negative symptoms I was having were related to the medication I was taking. It made me acutely aware of the effects medication can have, and it drove me to be more aware of the effects of medication when working with my clients. When they came into my office, and they were saying they have such and such a symptom, I would ask about their medication. I would look it up on the internet, and would tell the client if their symptom could be a side effect. If so, I would tell them to go back and talk to their doctor or psychiatrist, because I can't tell a person to stop taking a medication. My own awareness, mindfulness, and conscious use of self helped me to educate and empower my clients by teaching them to advocate for themselves.

A Pathway from Medicine to Motherhood to Social Work: Finding My Way

Nadine Bean, PhD, LCSW

PhD: Case Western Reserve University

MSSA (equivalent to MSW): Case Western Reserve University

BA: Biology and Psychology, Case Western Reserve University

Social Work Pathway and Work Experience

Nadine Bean, PhD, LCSW

Originally, I did not plan on becoming a social worker. I wanted to be a family medicine or child psychiatry physician. I was accepted to medical school and went for the first two years. When it was time for the clinical years with more than 100 hours in a work week, I decided there was a different path for me, especially because I had a young daughter with medical issues, and I wanted to be available for her care. However, I felt guilty about leaving medical school because it was so hard to get in, and I had taken up a space for two years.

I decided to go for counseling to help me sort through my feelings and figure out my next steps. The counselor turned out to be a licensed clinical social worker! I also remembered how much I loved Tuesday mornings in medical school because we were put into small groups to discuss how to build relationships with patients and hone our bedside manner, and other clinical skills. The small groups were co-facilitated by social workers and primary care physicians. I realized I was influenced a great deal by social workers and that it was my calling.

Eventually, I applied to the master's degree program in social work at Case Western Reserve University in Cleveland, Ohio, and never looked back! I became so passionate about social work that I decided I would like to teach at the master's level. The only way to accomplish this goal was to get a PhD.

When I first started, I thought I wanted to go into private practice, but I found my heart was in public service and public practice. I worked at a rural community mental health center in Ohio. I felt very at home with the community because my own family roots were in rural West Virginia. I understood the people we served, and I loved being in the rural communities.

When I was still working on my dissertation, my family relocated to the East Coast, and I got a job with the Baltimore County Early Intervention Program. My caseload consisted of families with children from birth to five years old who had developmental delays or disabilities. I provided emotional support services to the parents and caregivers to help them through the grief process people go through when they learn a child is not going to grow up in quite the way they dreamed and might have limitations and challenges. I considered much of the work I did with families to be grief and emotional support work.

Primarily, I worked with mothers. Even when fathers were in the picture, they rarely participated in the counseling. I also worked with grandparents raising grandchildren. I led groups for parents, caregivers, grandparents, and siblings of children with special needs. I loved every single second of it. Frequently, I found I was almost reparenting the parent or caregiver when I made home visits. I would demonstrate how to use play in engaging a child with different abilities and realized that many of these parents had never really been played with or nurtured well in their own childhoods.

After finishing my PhD and while still working in early intervention, I got a job as an adjunct professor at the University of Maryland School of Social Work, where I taught child welfare, family therapy, and social research methods. Then an opportunity came along for a one-year postdoctoral fellowship researching family violence in the military. I applied for the fellowship and got it! I was the first postdoctoral fellow at the University of Maryland School of Social Work. This was funded jointly by the Institute for the Advancement of Social Work Research, the Air Force, and the university. I primarily interviewed both social workers who worked with families in the Air Force and families that struggled with family violence and had received assistance from the social workers in the Family Advocacy Centers on bases.

Toward the end of the fellowship, I learned that West Chester University of Pennsylvania was starting a Master of Social Work program, and they were looking to hire. They wanted people to teach the advanced practice course with families, a child welfare elective, and advanced social research methods. These were all courses I had taught, so I applied. I was one of the first six faculty members hired for the new MSW program in 1998, which was very exciting! When I started as an academic, I vowed to never be the type of professor who hadn't seen a client in twenty-five or thirty years. Somehow, I wanted to also continue in direct service.

After September 11, 2001, I called the American Red Cross on September 12th and asked, "How can I help?" Little did I know quite a bit of training goes into becoming a Disaster Mental Health Services volunteer. I took an intensive three-day training on disaster response in general, disaster mental health services, and shelter operations offered by the American Red Cross. I learned how the Red Cross operates, the lingo, and the various roles people play. I became a Certified Disaster Mental Health Services volunteer, and my first assignment was in Lower Manhattan the beginning of January 2002, just after the holidays.

That was an incredibly critical time post-disaster. There are phases of a disaster, although they are not set in stone. People can move back and forth between stages. At the very beginning, people are in survival mode and in shock. Soon afterward is the honeymoon phase, which brings an outpouring of offers of aid, volunteers rushing in, and donations. When I volunteered, the honeymoon phase was fading, and people were facing the reality of all the destruction and loss in Lower Manhattan. The subway was not running, stores weren't open, restaurants had closed, taxi drivers lost their livelihoods, and all kinds of other supportive services were in turmoil. It was a critical time with a lot of emotional needs and despair. It was very depressing for people trying to get their lives back in order.

In 2005 after Hurricane Katrina devastated New Orleans, I also volunteered, mostly in the Lower Ninth Ward of New Orleans where the levees had broken. The flooding was unbelievable. Close to 100 percent of structures were unlivable or destroyed. By 2006, the Red Cross was no longer deploying disaster mental health volunteers in person because it is a disaster relief organization that helps for usually no more than six months. It is not a rebuilding organization. During my 2007 spring break, I Googled "volunteer opportunities in New Orleans," and I found a fledgling group led by both old and new "hippies" in the Lower Ninth Ward. They had a community center, community kitchen, and tool-lending library and were beginning to help clean up and rebuild homes. This was the predecessor to the organization I helped cofound, lowernine. org. During fall break 2007, I took a group of MSW students to help rebuild in the Lower Ninth Ward. During school breaks between 2007 and 2013, I took more than 100 students, some faculty, and staff from West Chester University to help rebuild.

I continued as a Disaster Mental Health Services volunteer for twenty years until it became too much for me to respond in person to either local or national disasters at all hours of the day and night.

Over the years, especially after doing my postdoctoral fellowship with the Air Force, and after 9/11, when I began volunteering with the Red Cross's Service to the Armed Forces, I developed a passion for working with veterans and military families, so I created an elective course called Social Work with Veterans and Military Families to help social work students develop the knowledge and skills needed to work with this population.

One of the highlights of my career at West Chester University was when I applied for a federal grant through the Department of Health and Human Services in the fall of 2017. We were awarded a Behavioral Health Workforce grant of $1.9 million to use over four years for MSW and MEd, School Counseling students. The grant provided $10,000 stipends to more than 100 students during their final year of internship to train them in the integrated healthcare model.

Integrated healthcare settings include primary care professionals (physicians, nurses, physician assistants) and mental health professionals, and sometimes other professionals such as registered dietitians, or occupational and physical therapists all under one roof. Often, when patients come in with symptoms such as a stomachache or sleeplessness, there might also be something going on emotionally. Most mental health issues first present in the primary care setting. Traditionally, the healthcare provider makes a referral to a mental health professional, but many times barriers prevent the person from getting the necessary mental health care. On the other hand, the integrated healthcare approach provides an opportunity for what is known as the warm handoff, so a patient can get mental health care right in the primary care provider's setting and not have to wait months for another appointment in a different setting.

I was very proud of this achievement! After twenty-two years of passionately teaching MSW students at West Chester University, I retired in 2020.

Self-Care Tips

I learned a great deal about self-care through my volunteer work with the Red Cross in Disaster Mental Health Services. The Red Cross has built-in requirements for taking care of our emotional, spiritual, and physical selves. The Red Cross made us take every fifth day off when working for 10 days or more at a large disaster site, such as after 9/11 or post-Hurricane Katrina. We could also reach out to other Disaster Mental Health Services volunteers who weren't deployed to talk about our experiences.

Still, because the work was so intense, sometimes I had nightmares. Two things I did to cope were journaling and writing poetry.

Practice Wisdom and Advice

- Work to dispel social work myths. For example, licensed social workers deliver about two-thirds of the mental health services in this country. There are more professional social workers in the country than psychologists, psychiatrists, professional counselors, and marriage and family therapists combined. Many people think only psychiatrists and psychologists provide these services.
- Uphold our central values. I hold them near and dear to my heart: The person-in-environment perspective, self-determination to the extent possible, the inherent dignity and worth of every single human being, the expectation that we advocate for social justice, and starting where the client is.
- Be flexible and versatile. This allows you to work with individuals, families, groups, organizations, or communities. Also, you can get involved in social policy at the local, state, or national governmental level. We even have social workers who are in Congress. Micro practice (at the individual and family levels) informs macro practice (organizations, communities, and governmental work) and vice versa.

Final Thoughts

Volunteering is very fulfilling. I continue to volunteer with Give an Hour, a volunteer network of licensed mental health professionals across the country who provide at least one hour a week of counseling to veterans and military families. I mostly work with clients who are dealing with post-traumatic stress. In my new hometown in the Lehigh Valley, Pennsylvania, I volunteer with Resilient Lehigh Valley. We provide education and training to professionals and lay audiences about the impact of trauma on lifelong health. I became the chair of the training action team, and I've made it my mission for our trainings to live up to the title of the organization. I'm determined that our trainings provide messages of hope and ways to build resilience.

I am grateful for my grounding in the medical and biological sciences because it helped me understand the mind-body connection.

I can't think of a profession so diverse, versatile, and impactful. I am so proud to be a social worker.

Making a Difference

Rachael Yudt, LCSW

MSW: Marywood University

BA: Penn State University

Social Work Pathway and Work Experience

My pathway began with a goal of getting a PhD in clinical psychology. My undergraduate degree was in psychology from Penn State in State College, Pennsylvania. When my husband started graduate school at the University of Rochester in New York, I started working at the University of Rochester, Mt. Hope Family Center in research that included transgenerational maltreatment in low socio-economic status families, lower education, or uneducated families. I would go to homes

Rachael Yudt, LCSW

and conduct demographic, mental health, and social determinants of health assessments of the family. I started to realize what I wanted was to have more "boots on the ground" impact in creating change. I heard stories of how systems failed families, and I needed to learn how to navigate systems and be an advocate for change in the various systems that continued to keep families where they are. That is when I changed my direction from getting a PhD in clinical psychology and doing research and teaching to having my "boots on the ground," which meant getting an MSW.

I started my social work degree at Syracuse University in New York and finished at Marywood University in the Berks County, Pennsylvania, Program with Alvernia University and the Lehigh Valley Program in Center Valley, Pennsylvania. I was working in the field at Caron Treatment Centers (addiction treatment and behavioral healthcare) doing intervention and prevention work with adolescents while studying for my MSW and during my field placements.

My field placements started my career trajectory. My first field placement was with a State Representative in Montgomery County, Pennsylvania, which introduced me to human trafficking. During my field placement I received an email asking to support a State Senator in recognizing Human Trafficking Awareness Day. This caught my attention, and I started researching and reading about human trafficking. I was doing work in schools with teens who had high Adverse Childhood Experience (ACE) scores, and I realized they were vulnerable. More importantly, I recognized that some of the teens with whom I worked were already being groomed or were already being exploited and trafficked. I dove more into learning and understanding the connection between traumatic childhood events, substance use and abuse, and risk for being exploited and trafficked. I continued to ask questions, and the State Representative asked if I would be interested in attending and learning more at the United Nations. Of course, I jumped at the opportunity. The representative's son-in-law was the Deputy Officer of Peace Negotiations at the United Nations. We went to NYC to visit the United Nations, talk with officials, and have lunch with the State Representative, Deputy Officer of Peace Negotiations, and the Deputy Officer of Human Relations. When I asked, "What does a social worker like me do to impact human trafficking?" she said, "Don't underestimate the power of acting locally." About two weeks later I started to organize what would become the Montgomery County Anti-Human Trafficking Coalition.

My next placement was with a social worker named Chuck G. who did police social work and domestic violence work. This was my exposure in understanding the offending side of domestic violence. He developed the "Safe Program," which worked with perpetrators of domestic violence and violence within their intimate relationships. I remember asking him, "How do you do this work and want to work with people who are purposely hurting others?" He put it in perspective by asking me if I ever yelled or said something hurtful to anyone as a means to shut them down. Upon reflection and insight, of course I did. It was then he explained that we all sit on this continuum; it is a matter of where and repair and change. He was a true advocate and served victims and survivors, and impacted change for many men who committed acts of violence to those they loved. He was a true mentor to me. This field experience brought my previous field experience full circle. I heard more stories of childhood traumatic experience and started to see the interwoven web of how systems and experience influence vulnerabilities to things like choosing abusive partners and to human trafficking. All systems are a part of our woven fabric and influence our understanding of ourselves and how we interact in the systems around us, including continuing to respond in a trauma response and creating core beliefs that perpetuate our traumatic experiences.

I always thought that I was going to go into macro work and was really interested in politics. Chuck taught me much about myself, empathy, and compassion. He taught me, "No matter who you work with, no one is far enough away from anyone to be immune to whatever you're doing." He taught me about yoga and Thich Nhat Hanh. He was like a father to me; the field lost a great man. I continue to use Chuck's influence in how I walk in this field, and in my understanding that language and approach to self and others are important.

I finished my MSW and started working in community mental health while remaining at Caron Treatment Centers. I was providing one-on-one mental health therapy to those with depression, anxiety, schizophrenia, and trauma alongside continuing to work with teens doing prevention and intervention substance and mental health work. When the school year ended in 2013, I started working at a safe house in Philadelphia for victims of human trafficking. These were people trying to survive and thrive. That's where I learned about trauma therapy. I loved that job, running the coalition and working with homeland security, the FBI, and local police departments. I was also hobnobbing with politicians because it became a very politically invested conversation and there was money to prevent human trafficking and support survivors.

Then I got tired of macro social work. I started to see why systems failed and became disenchanted with our political world.

I handed over the coalition to others and participated from afar, still involved but not leading. I also decided to leave my position in the city when my children became teenagers to spend more time with them. Knowing what I knew from my work, I recognized the importance of being home for them. That is when I started my own private practice, Anna's Hope, providing trauma therapy specializing in human trafficking and sexual exploitation. I named my practice after the first woman I worked with from rescue, safety, to thriving. I met her when I was leading the coalition. Homeland Security contacted me to work with them to get her to safety. I reached out to Anna at that time. She returned my phone call and we arranged a good time when we could talk. I called her back and she did not answer. A year later, almost to the day, I received a phone call from her, "I am ready." I transported her to Dawn's Place following an intake assessment over the phone. Once at Dawn's Place, I worked with her as her trauma therapist. She graduated from the program and was accepted into DePaul University School of Social Work in Chicago. She worked at getting some federal charges expunged and worked with the homeless population. Her traffickers were brought to justice, and she read her victim impact statement in front of her traffickers and the judge. She showed courage, bravery, strength, and dignity.

I remember the day she called me excited and a bit nervous about being accepted into DePaul's social work program. We talked about what her near future held, my support of her throughout her schooling, and the possibilities of her future. I talked about wanting to start my own gig and told her she could come work for me. She laughed and said, "No, you will work for me." I laughed and said, "Fair enough, you are the expert, you are smarter than me, and I will not only work for you, we can name our practice after you, Anna's Hope." She started to cry and asked if I would really do that. I said, "Of course." About three weeks before going to DePaul, she started having some strong trauma responses. We arranged for a meeting. I arranged for her to see the nurse practitioner and myself in the same day. This was a Monday at 7:30 p.m. About an hour after I left the message, I received a phone call from a colleague telling me that Anna overdosed and passed away. I decided that that was my moment to create Anna's Hope so I could keep my promise to her and provide space for her dream to help others live on. This was devastating and was the first significant loss of a client, someone who taught me how to hold space, how to see, hear, value, and care for someone who felt so broken. I cried many nights and helped her family clear out her apartment and talked with them about her healing.

I ran Anna's Hope for a while, teaching police officers and S.W.A.T. officers about human trafficking and trauma, educating community, and providing therapy and healing to those wanting to heal. I also offered trauma recovery yoga for my clients and for healthcare first responders. I used yoga, reiki, and boxing as modalities for treating trauma. I recognized, before somatic treatment was a big thing, that when you sit with someone who has extensive trauma responses to horrific events, particularly sexual traumatic events, they can't move fluidly, they hurt physically, they are stiff. This makes sense to me biologically.

I did this for a while until my husband became sick with cancer. I became the earner for the family. That is when I got into clinical supervision and company leadership. I worked in a partial hospitalization program while managing my husband's illness. I was a clinical supervisor, my husband's medical social worker, my children's support, and therapist. I managed this position while tending to being the primary caregiver to my husband and family through COVID. In November of 2020 my husband passed away, and I took FMLA to grieve and support our children. In December of 2020, I was offered a program manager position at Brandywine Hospital (owned by Tower Health) in Pennsylvania. It was a sixty-four-bed acute care hospital, including a geriatrics unit, an eating disorders unit, and two acute care units for psychiatric mental health issues. As the Program Manager, I led a staff of eighteen. We laughed, had fun, supported each other, cried together, and learned together. The highlight of my days was going onto the units, interacting with our patients, and watching the people I trained and supported in their work interact with them.

Unfortunately, systems fail, and Tower Health closed the hospital. I remember it was devastating for all the people who worked there, the patients, and their families. It was a true community mental health facility, and its closing was a huge loss for the community.

I received an offer at Pottstown Hospital, which is also part of Tower Health, for the position of Director of Behavioral Services for employee wellness. In response to the COVID-19 pandemic, they wanted to create programming to support staff because of the rate of burnout and people leaving their positions. I created a program to support staff across the board, including both employees and volunteers.

My job was to support people emotionally and give them skills to improve their mental health. I developed a pet therapy program for staff, supported a music therapy program for staff, and was working on developing an art therapy program. I also ran the critical incident and stress management team within the hospital. If there was a crisis, the CISM team dispersed and supported people who were affected by the crisis. After eight months, I had improved the retention rate by 20 percent. I then became one of the fifty-two middle management leaders they released—effective immediately. That never happened to me before, and it affected me greatly.

I took about six weeks off for self-reflection and rest and then accepted a position with a community mental health provider as the Clinical Coordinator. I supported therapists, providing supervision, and was back to a heavy therapeutic caseload. Because I am recognized as a Certified Clinical Trauma Professional and a comprehensive DBT trained therapist, I received a caseload of over fifty high-need clients. Following the passing of my husband and losing two jobs, I burned out quickly. I also realized that I wanted to spend this part of my career lending my understanding and knowledge to programming and teaching up-and-coming social workers how to use themselves as catalysts for micro and mezzo change.

I began talking with the CEO of Haven Behavioral Health Hospital, who had also worked at Tower Health, about Haven Behavioral Health building a brand-new hospital in West Chester, Pennsylvania. I am now the Executive Director of Clinical Operations, building my team and programs. We will be a seventy-two-bed acute care hospital with a step-down partial hospitalization, intensive outpatient program, and community group support.

I am excited about starting from scratch, creating the programs, and leading the staff with respect, care, and empathy. I don't want people to leave the profession because they are burned out, overworked, or underappreciated.

I recognize that in administration, revenue must be generated, and I respect that, or we will not have jobs. I truly believe there's a way to marry a positive work environment and revenue. The workplace does not have to feel adversarial.

Self-Care Tips

For self-care, I don't pressure myself to perform or meet expectations. I let things go as they go. I meet deadlines and plan, but I don't pressure myself to have expectations that may or may not be attainable. I set intentions.

I go to yoga, and I meditate. I walk my dogs every day. I take care of my body. I spend time with my friends. I spend time in nature. I also make sure that work for me is serious, yet I make sure that my team and I laugh a lot.

Rachael Yudt, LCSW, in Bir, India

A few years ago, I was fortunate to go to India for fifteen days, traveling light and nomadically, to study the Tibetan philosophy of living and dying. Part of our travels included staying in the same community as the Dalai Lama's home. We took daily morning kora (prayer) walks and were part of the Dalai Lama's teaching in his temple. Lama Pema took our things and had them blessed by the Dalai Lama, which was special. We went on hikes with Buddhist monks and nuns, praying and meditating in caves in the Himalayan Mountains.

It was the most enlightening part of my personal and professional life. The incidents of mental health issues and substance use are low in Northern India amongst people who had terrible things happen that caused them to leave their country. I believe that is because they live in the present moment, grounded and mindful, and meditate. The sense of community support was also strong. I brought these teachings back to my work, and it's how I lead others. This was a very powerful experience for me.

Today, we are implementing one- to three-minute meditations throughout the hospital, on the overhead speakers for the whole hospital three times a day, among other holistic practices for staff and guests.

Practice Wisdom and Advice

- Supervise. I think supervision is important not just for the supervisee, but also for the supervisor because I learn so much from the people I supervise—probably more from them than they do from me at times. We all need to be challenged and supported. It offers those being supervised an opportunity reflect and be more objective. It also offers them space to explore how they are affected by treating others.
- Learn from everyone. Continuing education is important to learn new ideas and mindsets. Continuing education allows for resetting, adding more to our toolbox, and making connections with others. Learning from client populations I work with and hearing their clinical stories and how they

approach situations gives me new thoughts and ideas while I share my thoughts and ideas with them clinically.

Final Thoughts

My strength in social work is that I connect with other people and really hear them and see them without judgment. I also understand that boundaries and limits are there to protect the client and us. Anna taught me that in a lot of ways. Being able to share yourself with someone, connect with them, and realize there is a fluid line in the relationship is powerful. Most important is our humanness together.

When you talk about the cycle of or progression of social work and the number of jobs and transitions you can do as social workers, I secretly brag to myself and to others because we are trained to pivot through all the different roles and settings. I went from macro to mezzo, to micro to mezzo.

If I can contribute anything to the social work profession, it is to know you're not destined to work in a closet with piles of paper around, sitting at a broken desk, on a broken chair. We deserve a brand-new office and a brand-new desk and chair because we keep our feet on the ground, and we put our hands out to people whom other people won't embrace.

Culture, Values, and Passion

Beatriz Sanabria Messina, LCSW

MSW: Marywood University

BSW: Cedar Crest College

Social Work Pathway and Work Experience

After graduating from high school, I did not know what I wanted to do. Two big things inspired me to pick social work as a career. The first thing was sort of self-serving. I don't want to be morbid and dramatic, but I started to think about the end of my life and my funeral. I thought, *When people are gathered there, hopefully a lot of people, what would I want them to think and say about me as they're saying their goodbyes? They could say, "She had a lot of material possessions and financial success. Look at all the things that she accumulated." Or do I want them to say, "She made a difference. She at least tried to leave the place better than she found it. She left this planet a little bit better."*

Beatriz Sanabria Messina, LCSW, serving as Marshal at Northampton Community College's Spring Commencement in 2018 (photo by Randy Monceaux)

The latter really appealed to me. If I am to be remembered for anything, I would like to be remembered for doing good and helping others. So I asked myself, *What profession does that?* I realized it is social work.

The second thing that inspired me to pick social work as a career was my family background, what my family had gone through. When I was twelve, my mother and I came to the United States from Costa Rica. We went from being in the racial majority to being in the racial minority. We went from being in the middle class because we had our own house with a yard to being poor. We went from knowing the language to not knowing the language.

The first thing that happened when we landed in the United States was my mother's purse got stolen. We ended up sleeping on the floor of the home of a nice elderly couple from South America who had seen what had happened at the airport. They opened their doors to us and let us sleep there for about a week. We then wound up staying in a shelter for battered women that was run by Catholic nuns, even though my mother wasn't a battered woman. We did not have the address of where we had planned to go nor much money because part of the money and the address were in my mother's purse.

Eventually, after my mother was able to contact my aunt back home, we made it to Allentown, Pennsylvania, which was our intended destination because my mother knew somebody who knew somebody there. I saw my mother struggle in the United States. In Costa Rica, my mother had worked in banks and offices and wore nice clothes to work. Here she had to take jobs in sweatshops, literal sweatshops. When she had to go to the restroom, the forewoman would watch her to make sure she didn't spend too much time in the bathroom because she was on the clock. It was not a good experience. As new immigrants, we received social services from places like the Hispanic American Organization (HAO) and Casa Guadalupe. We had free English classes, and I went to Catholic school on a scholarship.

My grandmother was important to me because she instinctively knew education was necessary to get ahead. She did not have much education and worked very hard. It was ingrained in me from the time I was a small child that education was critical. Hearing the stories about all the struggles that she went through, I thought, *Wow, if there had been social workers at that time to help my grandmother and grandfather, they could have moved their family (my mom, aunt, and uncle) forward with much less struggles.* And so, being an immigrant combined with my family history and knowing my grandmother's struggles motivated me to want to be a social worker. I couldn't help my grandparents since they were long gone, but I could maybe help other people.

My career began when I was attending community college to earn an associate's degree. I got into the field by getting a job as a case manager working with HIV-positive methadone maintenance patients. This led me to work in the substance use disorder field. I mainly worked in outpatient settings. I also did mental health counseling because they go hand in hand. At times, I was working at both or one or the other, but mainly in the drug and alcohol field. I received my bachelor's degree in social work (BSW) from Cedar Crest College, and my master's in social work from Marywood University. I most recently obtained my clinical license in social work in 2023.

I have been working at Northampton Community College (NCC) in Bethlehem, Pennsylvania, for more than ten years in the counseling department. Something I am most proud of is creating NCC's Collegiate Recovery Program (CRP) for students in recovery to support each other academically and in their recovery. This program helps to change the narrative and alleviate the stigma of addiction so students can feel welcomed and supported.

One of my most challenging experiences as a social worker was a situation when I had to really examine my personal values. The situation occurred when a client died. I was running a group of five or six men in Spanish at an outpatient drug and alcohol facility. We met weekly, so they could discuss their personal lives, struggles, and recovery. They helped each other to avoid falling into relapse. One day, a young man in his early twenties who was part of the group did not show up. I was a bit concerned, but I thought maybe he missed the bus or something. A few days later, I received a phone call from his probation officer, who told me that the young man died of an overdose. I was heartbroken. It was just terrible. It wasn't the first time I lost a client, but it's always terrible.

I talked with my supervisor about how to handle this with the group. As the group and I were processing, they started to tell me they were concerned about this young man before this happened due to his behavior. Being in the drug and alcohol field, one quickly learns that clients are really good at noticing other people's behaviors. When other people are doing things wrong, they can pick it up very, very quickly. It's hard for somebody who suffers from a substance use disorder to fool another person who is dealing with these issues. They had their concerns about this young man, and one of them had even seen him in an area of town that's known as a place to go to get drugs. I was completely shocked that none of them had said anything to the young man. They didn't pull him aside nor let me know their concerns.

As I was processing all this, I said, "Someone could have left a note on my chair about your concerns. You didn't have to identify yourself. Someone is dead, gone forever, and you were worried and concerned about him."

They said, "We knew it, and we saw him here, and he was not acting right."

My brain was exploding as they told me, and I said, "Nobody did anything."

Their response was, "Snitching on someone is the ultimate no-no."

I realized that is a powerful drug culture value. Even though they knew something was wrong, not telling on someone was more important than the value of a person's life. I was distraught and talked to my supervisor to help me process everything. From my views and values, I felt his death could have been prevented. What I learned from my supervisor was that the value of not telling overrode the possibility of saving the person's life. This was so contrary to my personal and professional values because life is important to me. So my values were in conflict with those of my clients. This is a difficult situation in practice, and it presented an ethical dilemma for me.

Self-Care Tips

Self-care is a challenge, yet so important. Currently, what I do on a regular basis is exercise, so I am moving my body. That's big. I became a Zumba instructor and love teaching Zumba classes. I love the dancing, and it incorporates a lot of Latin music, so I feel I am sharing my culture with people when I am teaching. I also like to take exercise classes and am willing to try any kind of exercise class at least once. I also love to run.

Two and a half years ago, I started learning how to play the violin. Practicing violin makes me take time for myself. You can't rush and do it quickly, so you must dedicate time, and I feel good about my progression. It also reminds me that I am capable of accomplishing difficult things.

The latest thing I've picked up as a form of self-care and stress reliever is cake decorating! I love to bake, and cake decorating allows me to be creative because I get to design how I want the cakes to look. I've been at it for about a year now. I enjoy the challenge of perfecting the cakes, and I am willing to take my time. I enjoy giving them as gifts.

I also am a very social, outgoing person. I love being with people, especially my husband and the rest of my family, which includes my mom, my aunt, and my two stepdaughters.

Practice Wisdom and Advice

- Volunteer! If you think you might want to work in a particular area, try volunteering to see if it is for you or get an entry-level job like I did as a case manager. Get your foot in the door.
- Try to keep the empowering nature of

Beatriz Sanabria Messina, LCSW, serving as Mistress of Ceremonies at the Latino Leadership Alliance of the Lehigh Valley Fundraising Gala in 2022 (photo by John Kish IV)

social work in the forefront of your mind. I feel very empowered being a social worker, and I see it as a superpower. Not only do you become empowered as a social worker, but also you learn to teach others to be empowered. Your clients learn by watching the way you conduct yourself, and I always remind my clients that they have agency. You have more power than you think you have.

- Implement self-care, especially for people just coming into the profession because it can be a routine that you develop and carry throughout your career and your life. If you start something early, it could become a lifelong habit. Make sure to remember your mental, emotional, and physical well-being.

- There is a lot of pain in the world, so keep in mind you cannot help everyone in every situation.

- Know you are not alone. There are many other helping professionals we can seek for guidance.

- Also, remember what you do, no matter how small at times, does make a difference. Even a smile at the right time can make a huge difference. You have the ability. You are capable.

Final Thoughts

One of the wonderful things about social work is you get to do so many different things, and you can wear many different hats.

Starting supervision for your clinical license as soon as you can is wise if that's your goal. You can have doors open to you. If you want to have your own

Beatriz Sanabria Messina, LCSW, serving as race director at Northampton Community College's seventh annual Spartan Sprint 5K Run/Walk in 2021 (photo by Carlo Acerra)

93

practice, don't wait. See if the place where you are going to be employed or are employed has someone with a license who can supervise you. If not, start paying someone right away so you don't delay the clinical licensure process.

Look for mentors and test out areas of practice you think might be of interest. Knowing early on the populations that you are not suited well for will move you in the direction of your strengths. If it doesn't work, just leave it. Concentrate on what you are passionate about and the population that you are amazing with or that you really want to work with.

Sometimes we do not know the impact we make. Once, I met with a client and didn't feel I had done anything remarkable in our session together. Later that day, I received a voicemail from her, thanking me for taking time to meet. I wondered what I had done and realized that just being present, listening, and allowing her to share her story was what she needed.

A Michigan Region BBYO Legend

Arnie Weiner, MSW

MSW: University of Michigan

BA: University of Michigan

Social Work Pathway and Work Experience

It is interesting to reflect about what made me become a social worker. My mother thought I should be an accountant because I was so good at detail, but I said, "Mom, that sounds so boring." I started at Grand Rapids Junior College and after getting my Associate in Arts degree there, I matriculated into the University of Michigan School of Literature,

Arnie Weiner, MSW (2010)

Science & Arts, majoring in political science with a minor in history. I also worked toward a teaching certificate from the School of Education and did student teaching. I began to realize I was more interested in working with young people than teaching them civics.

At the same time, I lived in a co-op house in Ann Arbor. There were a lot of guys in the co-op, and some of them were studying at the School of Social Work. They would sit and talk to me about what they were doing and how much they enjoyed the work. It sounded exciting to me. At that point, I decided social work seemed to be more in my interest than teaching.

I applied to the U of M School of Social Work, and to my delight, I got accepted. I spent the next two years getting my Master of Social Work degree, with a major in Community Practice and a minor in Group Work. It turned out to be the best two years of my education because of the students, professors, small class size, and field placements. I was able to "do something" as opposed to just sitting in a classroom.

I loved community practice, and my first field placement was with Neighborhood Services Organization in Brewster-Douglas public housing in Detroit. My second placement was at United Community Services in Windsor, Ontario. I worked with block clubs of residents in both places, working to achieve goals for felt needs.

The night that Martin Luther King Jr. was killed, one of the paraprofessionals with whom I worked asked me, "Arnie, why do you work down here?" I said, "Well, because I want to help develop the community and give people an opportunity to advance." She said, "But you're Jewish, and you should be working in your community." She accompanied me to my car and got me out of there because she was afraid of what might happen that night.

At the beginning of my second year at SSW, Dr. Jack Rothman (a U of M social work professor) called me into his office. I was very active in the Social Work Student Union, so he knew me. He asked, "You're Jewish, aren't you?"

When I said yes, he responded, "Well, I have an opportunity for you. Beth Israel Synagogue in Ann Arbor is looking for an adult advisor for the B'nai B'rith Youth Organization (BBYO) chapter." I grew up in Grand Rapids and was very involved in BBYO, so I said, "That sounds great. I would love to help out." I took the advisor position from 1968 to 1969. I loved working with the teens, and they loved working with me. During that year, I staffed several conclaves with the teens, and evidently, I was observed by Manny Mandel, who was the director of Michigan BBYO at that time.

In the spring of 1969, when I was ready to graduate, Manny approached me and said, "You know, I have an Assistant Director position open, and I think you'd be good for it." Frankly, I did not know what was going to happen, as I had lost my student deferment that year and was being pursued by Selective Service (for an expense-paid trip to Vietnam), and I was exploring other employment opportunities as well. I thought that if I took a position out of town, I'd have to move and then in a few months I might have to go into the service. (It turned out that my eyesight was so poor that I didn't pass my physical.) The idea of taking the job in Detroit without having to move gave me more flexibility.

I took the job, and Manny became my mentor and supervisor. He was Hungarian-born and a Holocaust survivor. I learned a great deal from him because he was very disciplined and provided ongoing, regular supervision. We didn't always see eye to eye and argued a good deal because he had a European disposition about things, and I had a young American perspective. We still loved and respected each other and recognized that there were times we would agree to disagree. I stay in touch with him to this day, and he is in his mid-eighties! In fact, he recently was among the Holocaust survivors invited to the Chanukah candle-lighting at the White House with President Biden.

One thing that stands out is that in my first year Manny told me that he was recommending me to lead a three-week teen tour to Israel. "It will enhance your Jewish perspective and change your whole life." When I came back in the summer of 1970, I let Manny know that it had definitely changed my life and opened my eyes. It became very important for me to try to get as many teens as possible to Israel as part of their learning experience. Those three years with Manny meant a great deal to me.

In 1973 Manny took a position in the BBYO International Office in Washington and recommended me to be the Director of Michigan BBYO. By that time, I knew I had a certain way of working with teens, and they loved working with me as well. I felt that this was a program I could develop and make even better. As a child of the sixties, I was very service-oriented. JFK's slogan, "Ask not what your country can do for you; ask what you can do for your country," rang true for me. I took the job.

I have watched many colleagues over the years move to other organizations with more prestige and higher pay, as they saw BBYO as a "starting place" to gain experience. I saw BBYO as a career. I believed that the kids deserved people who cared about them and their development, and I felt that I was one of those people. I got involved in helping form a BBYO Staff Association and then a BBYO Staff Union so people could make BBYO their career. I became active in the Union, eventually becoming President, and helped create a career ladder with sizeable wage and benefit increases. This made it easier for someone to stay, since the agency was able to respond to our financial needs.

Treating teens with respect and listening to them was critical. To this day, I love bumping into former BBYO members and seeing their growth and the impact BBYO had on their lives. The status of the agency grew, and people in the community began to know and trust me.

In Social Work School, group work was a minor for me. My philosophy as BBYO Director was that "every teen needs to be confronted with the choice of joining or not joining BBYO." In other words, I directed my staff toward outreach, making the organization more well-known in each area high school. When a teen joined, he/she became part of a small group called a "chapter." These chapters met weekly and provided the teens with the opportunity for leadership development, fostering life-long friendships, and choosing and planning programming that was relevant to them. If the chapters were a nice place to be, teens would bring their friends to meetings and relationships would be formed.

One of my biggest joys was creating new chapter groups. Our region had up to forty chapters and more than 1,000 teens each year. In my thirty-nine years as Director, I estimated that around 41,000 teens were part of BBYO! We also fo-

On the phone in the Negev on Detroit Teen Mission (1997)

98

cused on leadership training, community service, exploring one's Jewish heritage, and learning how to democratically run a chapter and the region, where officers were elected by the teens. We were teaching life skills.

I had amazing staff over the years who helped make Michigan Region strong. Providing them with ongoing, regular supervision was something to which I was very committed. If I could train them to do their job better, I wouldn't have to do it for them. My staff really appreciated this attention, and we became quite a team. One of my past assistants recently wrote to me, "I often think fondly of the time I worked at BBYO with you. It felt like family. There was such a sense of support and collaboration that I've not experienced any place else that I have worked."

I felt great satisfaction that I was able to make a difference in these kids' lives, so my life was worthwhile because of that. It was a fun job, I loved my work, and I always had passion for what I was doing. One of the biggest accomplishments in my time was to achieve recognition for BBYO in the community and acceptance as an agency of the Jewish Federation, because this was an important funding source. They began to allocate money to us, helping to fund staff positions. It also allowed me, as an Agency Director, to attend meetings with other Jewish community organization professional staff. This raised BBYO's status in the community tremendously.

Another accomplishment that was important to me was making sure funding was available for teens to participate in summer leadership experiences. I was able to approach many wonderful alumni, with whom I maintained ongoing contact and who had strong feelings about their experience in the program, and we established scholarship funds for each of several leadership, Judaism, and Israel travel programs.

Later in my career, I was appointed to the BBYO National Management team and given the responsibility of supervising other regions. I used to fly to Milwaukee, Chicago, Toronto, and Montreal, helping as much as I could. I tried to be respectful of the people whom I supervised and understand what they were up against. In 1999, I was asked to serve as the Interim BBYO International Director for a year. I was hesitant to accept because I wanted to make sure I could still be the Michigan BBYO Director as I would also have to spend some time in Washington, D.C. I enjoyed the year but knew that Detroit was my home and where I wanted to be.

I remain passionate about BBYO and was recently honored at a dinner where more than 275 people attended (alumni from as far back as 1969, former staff, parents, Jewish Federation and B'nai B'rith leaders)! For me, staying in the same job for my career helped me build the program, create lasting friendships, be trusted in the community, and impact many lives.

Self-Care Tips

- You can only do so much and do it well!
- If it is to be, it's up to me!
- Excellence is never an accident.

Practice Wisdom and Advice

- Know that people with social work degrees can do so many things these days. When I was in school, I do not think we conceptualized the breadth of how you could use your degree and the many practice areas you could

Arnie on the streets of Plovdiv, Bulgaria, in January 2002

explore. I encourage people to look around and see what's out there.
- Keep in mind how you feel and question if what you are doing is fulfilling. Think about if you enjoy the people you are working with, what you want to accomplish

professionally, and whether or not you are getting paid so you can live comfortably. I looked forward to coming to work every day. Do you? Make sure to love what you are doing and that you are contributing to society in some way.
- Find a job where you can use your social work skills.
- Remember that being passionate about your work is key.
- One of my favorite sayings about leadership:
  A leader is best
  When people barely know that he/she exists
  But of a good leader, who talks little,
  When his/her work is done, his/her aim fulfilled,
  They will say, "We did this ourselves."

Final Thoughts

Our work lends itself well to volunteering even after you have retired. I had the pleasure of working with so many wonderful volunteers over the years, both chapter advisors as well as members of our Board. They became terrific role models for me. When I retired, I decided I still wanted to be involved in the community. I'm on the Board of my synagogue as a Vice President. I am also the editor of the monthly

Arnie Weiner, MSW, at BBYO 1970's reunion (2019)

synagogue newsletter. I use the skills I developed working for BBYO in these positions. I also volunteer at Yad Ezra, the Jewish food bank in our community, and for the Great Lakes Chamber Music Festival. Volunteering is important. It keeps me involved in the community and allows me to express my values.

Challenges, Change, and Continued Learning

Susan McDonald, PhD, LCSW
PhD: Fordham University
MSW: Marywood University
BA: King's College

Social Work Pathway and Work Experience

When I went to King's College in Wilkes-Barre, Pennsylvania, I studied criminal justice and thought I wanted to work with juvenile delinquent kids. I was fascinated during my first internship at the Juvenile Detention Center in Wilkes-Barre, PA, because I could go to court and conduct home visits. The director of the center was a social worker and my first mentor. She was a fantastic person, and I was in awe of this busy woman who took the time to meet with me and teach me.

Susan McDonald, PhD, LCSW

Following that experience, I became a certified addiction counselor, and while doing this work, I became curious that addiction does not come alone. Usually, it is a result of trauma or some other issue. I got interested in mental health and then decided I needed more education. I investigated different graduate programs and talked to health-care and education professionals in my community who knew me well. They all suggested social work would suit me because I had always volunteered in the community. They felt service was a vital component of who I am as a human being, so they thought social work would be the perfect fit.

I knew nothing about social work, but I trusted the professionals who gave me advice. I applied to the Marywood School of Social Work and got accepted. After earning my MSW, I still wanted more and felt I needed to learn more by getting a PhD at some point.

I like a lot of challenges and changes. I can't just stay still! My work with people with addictions led me to work in community mental health.

One day, a colleague said, "My wife is a nurse, and they are always looking for social workers. Would you consider doing part-time social work in a home health agency?"

So, in addition to working full-time in community mental health with homeless people, many of whom had a diagnosis of schizophrenia, I added working weekends doing home healthcare, all while raising a family. I loved the challenges of working in community mental health, and the home healthcare was easy in comparison because I would get the client what they needed, such as medical equipment, chat for a bit, and then I was DONE!

The home healthcare agency owner, interested in opening a hospice, said, "I want you to be our social worker."

Okay, that's a nice challenge and a change. I went for the training, which was great, and started working in a hospice. That was the best job I ever had because it was intimate work. I'm always amazed that people invite you into their homes at one of the most challenging moments and they were willing to share their life experiences with me. It just really humbled me in so many ways, especially witnessing the dying process and being present with someone as they draw their last breath.

A professor at the University of Scranton asked me if I would present on death and dying to his class. At the end of the class, he said, "I never get these students to open up, and you just couldn't shut them up! They were so engaged. I think you need to go into teaching."

I thought about going into teaching, which confirmed what I needed to do next. I applied to Fordham University for my PhD and got accepted! The professor from the University of Scranton said they are always looking for adjunct professors at Marywood University in Scranton, Pennsylvania. I applied and got the teaching job while working on my PhD.

When I finished my PhD, I started teaching at DeSales University in Center Valley, Pennsylvania and maintained a small private practice. I needed both the clinical and education pieces. At this point, I had to let go of working for hospice. At DeSales, I was hired to get the social work program accredited. Due to a change in president and direction, they decided not to seek social work accreditation, so I had to find another job.

Eventually, I went to Alvernia College in Reading, Pennsylvania and became the director of the Social Work Program. I got hired because the director had died suddenly, and they needed somebody to fill in quickly. My hospice experience helped me because students were in a state of shock. I asked the president and the dean if they had addressed the sudden death and loss of this professor. They had not. So I did, and that helped pave the way for me to lead the program and through the accreditation process.

After some time at Alvernia, I wanted to work closer to my home in Kingston, Pennsylvania. I spent the past few years working in academia at Misericordia University in Dallas, Pennsylvania, where I was the social work program director. That is where I ended my teaching career. I continue with my private practice, which I thoroughly enjoy. I love narrative work, developed by Michael White and David Epston, that views clients as the experts of their lives. Narrative Therapy aligns well with my professional values. I like helping people share their stories.

Self-Care Tips

I have done many presentations about self-care ethics because it is unethical if you are not practicing self-care. Self-care must be integrated throughout your day and your life.

I do not see self-care as going for a manicure or a pedicure. I practice self-care by meditating every day. I also practice yoga daily.

Because I like to challenge and change and think intellectually, I find reading good books that stimulate thinking and going to lectures to be part of my self-care.

Being in nature is one of the best ways to practice self-care.

Self-care is also doing things for your mind, body, and soul that make you feel better and healthy as a human, such as getting proper rest, eating nutritious food, and having great friendships. Spiritual practices can also be an essential part of self-care.

Practice Wisdom and Advice

- Have supervision. Finding a supervisor with the time to meet with you at least one hour per week is essential. I wonder if agencies support this enough because of time constraints and other demands. If you want well-trained social workers, you must honor great supervisors. It's not a paid position, frequently not even recognized. So, you're asking many folks who are already incredibly busy. I think there needs to be more support in agencies for supervision.
- We live in a time of polarization, and the stakes are high. We need to come together quickly and purposefully to effect change. Social work is a community base that can bring people together.
- Value mentors. Mentors are your guides. You don't know what you don't know—having someone invested in you and your growth professionally and personally is essential. Mentors can teach you by sharing practice wisdom you do not learn in a classroom. It would help if you had the combination of academics and the wisdom those in practice provide. I have been fortunate to have mentors guide me on my path. My most important and unique mentor was Esther. She was the first social worker in our community to open a private practice, which was groundbreaking in many ways. Esther took me under her wing and taught me

much about social work practice. If you are lucky, mentors can become personal friends. Esther and I developed a friendship that lasted many years until her death.

- Build resiliency. I was doing a large presentation about employee assistance programs for a group of truck drivers. They practically booed me off the stage. I was sweating bullets, and when I got off the stage, I thought that was the worst experience of my life. When I spoke with another mentor about this experience, he said, "That is how you build resiliency. You don't learn anything when you hit it right out of the ballpark. When you get booed off the stage humiliated, you must brush yourself off and get back up again." His support and guidance stuck with me and helped me use this as a learning experience.

Final Thoughts

My life philosophy comes from Stoicism, a practical, reality-based approach to life. It is a valuable way of being and understanding the simplicity of life. The simple things in life drive me philosophically. I find it essential to integrate growth in my inner journey with my external journey, all with self-compassion and compassion for others. It is the importance of human relationships.

The workplace can be challenging and stressful. It is essential to have good colleagues to support you through difficult times. These relationships can become lifelong friendships.

If you are thinking about changing what you do in social work or are trying to figure out where to begin, find a starting point. One of my morning meditation readings is by Rolf Gates, a former Army Ranger who did map making. He said you must get an accurate starting point because if it's 3:00 am, pouring down rain, and your coordinates are off, you will never find a home base. Ever. The starting point is essential.

I love the idea of a starting point. We all need to sit down occasionally and get in touch with our starting point, including awareness of our values. Writing a brief mission statement can be powerful to guide you on your internal journey. We know things happen, such as workplace dilemmas, crises, etc., and it can be easy to get off course. Having an accurate starting point helps us reconnect with our values and clarifies our mission.

Self-knowledge is also crucial. I know that I need challenges and change. But only some do. I had a classmate who has worked in kidney dialysis for over thirty years and is still passionate about the work. So, we are all different and need to know ourselves.

Faith and Social Work Are My Platform

Sharon Rice, LSW, MSS/MLSP

MSS/MLSP: Bryn Mawr College Graduate School of Social
Services and Social Research

BA: Saint Joseph's University

Social Work Pathway and Work Experience

I graduated from Saint Joseph's University with an undergrad degree in psychology and had no clue what I wanted to do. I think most people can probably relate to that! I applied to lots of different positions, but I wasn't really getting a lot of traction.

Sharon Rice, LSW, MSS/MLSP

A friend of my mother's recommended I apply for a position at the Department of Youth and Family Services (DYFS) in New Jersey because they were doing a mass hiring. I had never heard of the agency and didn't really know anything about child welfare, so I went for an interview and completely misunderstood what the interviewers were asking.

They walked me through a case scenario and asked questions about how I would handle talking to the child. I did not realize that taking notes was allowed, so I spent the entire time memorizing everything! I had no clue what I was talking about, but they were so impressed with me, I was hired on the spot!

108

I worked at DYFS for four years, doing everything that I could do at the time, including ongoing case management, intake, and investigative work. I also worked in the centralized screening facility. That was my introduction to the world of social work and child welfare.

I didn't actively choose social work as my career. It was something I was encouraged to study based on things I told people about how I view the world and what I wanted to do to challenge myself in my career. One day, a friend who studied at Bryn Mawr back in the seventies suggested, "It's a great school and environment. Why don't you check it out?"

I was interested in systems change, working in the strategy space, and in nonprofit management versus direct service, so I went to see the school and liked the program. I graduated from Bryn Mawr with my Master of Law and Social Policy (MLSP) and my Master of Social Service (MSS) with a concentration in social service management. I knew I wanted to do more macro level work.

My first job after graduate school was Clinician at Community Treatment Solutions in New Jersey. I did individual therapy and some group therapy with youth who were placed in intensive therapeutic foster homes. I worked with a team, including a case manager and wrap-around services in conjunction with Children and Youth Services in that county. I discovered that although I'm a good therapist, I don't enjoy the process.

I left that position for a self-imposed sabbatical. I did a lot of exploring and networking in Philadelphia. I ended up at a nonprofit digital online communication platform called Generocity. The mission of Generocity was to share good news from the nonprofit world with the rest of the world. At that time, people were grabbing on to the idea of corporate social responsibility and helping to solve big world problems. As their Director of Community Relations, I did a lot of on-the-ground work talking with organizations, finding interesting stories, and figuring out where we could really get our hands into the meat of this work.

My next job was Clinical Facilitator at a domestic violence organization, doing adult education concerning abuse of women and men. I worked with men's and women's groups, and I led staff training. Our foundational training was a forty-hour training required for all people who work in domestic violence organizations. I did that for about three years. It was eye-opening to see the effects of domestic violence.

I also recognized the limitations for educating adults. Helping adults who experienced domestic violence hinges on whether or not they're willing to be a part of the service versus just getting the education. A lot more attention is given to youth. Although my work in domestic violence was fulfilling, I wanted to take another leap working at the macro level.

I took a position at Bethana in Philadelphia, a community umbrella organization working to strengthen families and promote resilience. When kids come into the system requiring ongoing services, such as foster care, they can get all those services within their neighborhood to keep their family intact and enable them to continue to go to their school. This way, the children are not taken out of what they know. I was a supervisor and started right before the COVID-19 pandemic. We worked a lot from home. I had an amazing group of case managers who were very dedicated to their work.

Child Protective Services had significantly changed since I worked in New Jersey. The law in Pennsylvania had advanced. Terms are defined more clearly and more succinctly, helping people to really understand what abuse is and what abuse is not. I did that job for about a year, and then a former colleague became the Executive Director of the Philadelphia Children's Alliance. She asked me to apply for an open Program Manager position. I applied, was hired, and found it was one of those situations that was practically too good to be true. That is where I currently work!

Self-Care Tips

My life philosophy that guides my work is that I am a Christian. It is not a religion, but a relationship with God, and I have accepted salvation. I went to Catholic school, so I had a sense that God was real, but I didn't have a personal connection for a long, long time. When I worked with abused kids, it kind of pushed me for understanding why abuse happens. My sister invited me to church because she discerned it would be good for me to have a relationship with God. It is good for folks to understand I live by a certain set of beliefs because the Bible is not really about rules— it's more about life itself. In terms of a philosophy, I think it's just me saying, *This is how I live, and my standard is Jesus Christ. He is the person I go after. He is the person that guides my vision, and I'm guided day to day on this journey by the Holy Spirit. I recognize I am created in God's image. Therefore, that means I am someone, an individual who has experienced my own hurts, my own traumas, my own disappointments. The peace and joy I get from knowing there's an eternity, and that there is a way out of things that doesn't require me to go and hurt somebody else is my life itself.* I am a believer, and it is saying to God, *Place me as a seal on your heart.* For me that means my identity is in you and your love is strong enough within me to carry on in this world where all these things are happening. My first instinct with anybody, with any job acquaintance, friendship, whatever it is, is to appreciate it through a lens of how God loves this person. If God is loving this person, I want to know how He's doing it, because I am a created being by Him and I want to love the way He loves. This belief helps me get through challenging situations.

I also have prayer and meditation time.

Practice Wisdom and Advice

- Network. Even when I was tired, I opted to go to events. I often went to events outside of my career field to gain a different perspective on life. I realized that the people I am servicing don't live in the same space that I live in, so their understanding of systems is much different from mine. I learned about systems as a practitioner, but they engage with systems as a client. The "system" is not just services. It is also the system of gaining employment and renting an apartment. Get to know what's going on in your community and your neighborhood. I recommend going to events once or twice a month.

- Don't begrudge the moments in your life when you don't have a mentor. I often didn't have one. Take those opportunities to say, "Okay, this is still a learning experience. When the time comes for me to find a mentor, I will have a list of things that I really am interested in and the things that I don't want to know about so that I can get to the place I want to be."

Final Thoughts

What I have found most challenging about social work is integrating my faith into my work without compromising my values. I do not disregard another person's identity because I understand that not everyone believes in God. It would be my prayer that everyone comes to know Jesus as their Lord and Savior. That's my prayer. That's the prayer for anybody who believes in Jesus. We would all accept Him. However, that's not the case, and that does not mean that a family or a child should not be serviced well, with excellence, with love, with care, and compassion. I think my biggest challenge has always been asking God, *How do I do this work as a believer, and knowing that there are things happening in the world that I don't believe in?* Sometimes I've had clients find out that I'm a Christian and challenge me in a very pointed way. There is this strange space of identifying as a Christian, but also a social worker. I can't live with these two worlds parallel. I realized that social work is my platform as a Christian. I think, *Okay, God, I can see why you give me social work as my platform. I can see why this is what you want me to do right now, and so let me not quit before the race is over.*

To people who have a faith life and are doing social work, I suggest getting comfortable with asking yourself and your faith community hard questions about how to do this work.

One thing that I wish I had done earlier in my career was to have hard conversations with people in my faith community about things that shock me. I always felt like that was taboo to discuss. Eventually, I realized these people could understand what I'm talking about and be helpful to me. I put my faith first, but I'm not going to dismantle another person's life just because my faith might not agree with their lifestyle or identity. My faith is the guide for how I interact with people, and social work is one of the platforms I've been given to engage the world.

A Unique Social Work Journey from the United States to Finland

Leigh Anne Rauhala, LCSW

MSW: University of Central Florida

BA: Psychology: University of South Florida

Social Work Pathway and Work Experience

Originally, I wanted to be a psychologist so I could counsel and work with people. One of my teachers played a pivotal role in altering my course when he advised me that psychology had become more focused on testing and evaluation. Definitely not my bag!

Leigh Anne Rauhala, LCSW

That advice gave me permission to reconsider my direction. That's when I discovered, with the help of my aunt Mary, that social work was a much better fit. I realized that money wasn't really a driver for my career. Rather I'm driven by my passion for helping people. Being a social worker is at my core.

Prior to social work, I worked in a surf shop in buying and accounting, and then I did a stint in banking. But my social work career began at a Community Mental Health Center (CMHC) in Orange County, Florida. I began as an on-site children's therapist at a residential foster care group home.

From there, I moved into the Assessment Center at the CMHC, to work as a Lead Assessment Specialist, working with clients with more chronic mental health issues and emergency acute care needs. Soon after, I moved into a supervisor role for two years. It was here that I really discovered how crucial accurate assessment work was. I could see the results that followed the person and my assessment of the presenting issues moving into other departments. I had to be detailed, and careful to gather the correct information. This is where I honed my strong listening skills. An assessment center is a great place to work if you like adrenaline and no two days alike!

My next step was as the Clinical Program Manager of Adult Case Management. The type of services varied between case managers checking in with their clients monthly to an Assertive Community Treatment model. This was meant to be a hospital without walls with services and on-call available 24/7 designed to keep clients out of the state hospital. I worked with an amazing team of nurses, therapists, a psychiatrist, and case managers to support people living in the community.

During all of this I was fortunate to have Peg as a mentor. She was my boss when I worked at the CMHC. She is the most loving and peaceful person who has a completely pragmatic view of the world even in the midst of chaos. She really helped me find balance as I tend to be more emotional in my interactions. She is now retired, still counseling, and luckily for me, we are still great friends. I think it is important to find a mentor—someone you respect and feel connected to. They help you to grow professionally. Mentoring is an important part of supervision in social work. If we do not have supervisors or mentors, we may find it difficult to see other perspectives, leading us to make the same mistakes repeatedly. Supervision helps us realize that while this work is hard and not black and white, it is rewarding and meaningful. Peg helped me to discover who I am as a social worker and who I am as an educator is directly tied to who I am authentically!

When I was still in the United States working at the CMHC, one of my career highlights was when the company bought an older hospital and remodeled and added inpatient care units.

One of the team leaders on my case management team was a pastor as well as a nurse, and together we lobbied to create a nondenominational prayer or quiet room out of one of the empty rooms. This was a big deal back then in terms of public services and social work because spirituality and social work were not generally discussed as complementary dimensions of services. We were trained not to bring our spirituality into the equation. However, spirituality is such a huge part of so many people's lives. Giving space and an opportunity for dialogue with people around mental health and social work, in general, was greatly needed. I want to emphasize that it was not my spirituality, but whatever spiritual practice or dimension the individual felt might be supportive in their life or situation.

While work was going gangbusters, my personal life was not. I ended up getting divorced, which gave me an opportunity to take a girls' trip to Europe with my mom and sister. We had never been off the American continent! While abroad, I met my future husband in Vienna at the symphony. We were married a year later, and I moved to Finland to be with him. What an adventure…no worries…social work career in six months, right?

Ha! The first couple of years were a challenge I never expected. Because I wasn't working at first, I experienced complete culture shock going from identifying as a Clinical Program Manager to a life where the biggest decision I made all day was what to make for dinner. Not to bash cooking, but I am definitely not a kitchen maven. The change caused me to ask myself questions such as "Who am I?" and "What is my purpose?" It took me a couple of years and a return to my faith foundations to realize I am not just my job. My purpose on this earth is to help people.

I began teaching English, then immersed myself in learning Finnish for a year. In Finland, as part of the integration system, I was paid to learn Finnish by the government. Once again, I had a paycheck!

I also became part of the American Women's Club and eventually became its President. After a couple of years, I decided it was time to get back into social work and got in touch with the local University of Applied Sciences. I asked how I could get a job in social work or if I should just take courses again as a way to build a network. Their response was, "How do you feel about teaching?" An American degree is highly valued in Finland, and I became an adjunct instructor for three years before I was hired full-time! Sixteen years later, I could not have dreamed up this life if I had tried!

Part of my evolution as a social worker has been moving away from having a very clinical viewpoint to a more holistic perspective of social work based on Social Pedagogy. In 2015, we started working with three other international universities from Ghent, Copenhagen, and Amsterdam to brainstorm around future educational needs and trends in social work over the next ten years. We agreed that urban social work is a place where we don't pay enough attention. Clinical social workers don't focus on this area. Our person-in-environment perspective often left out the physical, natural, and built environments we live in. We have become very case-based and individual-oriented in our work. To address this, together we created a thirty-credit joint semester, Social Work in Urban Areas, where students spend a semester in one of the cities and use it as a learning lab while the teachers "fly in" to teach their topics, which are cross-disciplinary as well as international. We got such good feedback from conferences and from colleagues that we decided we needed more research on these ideas, so we applied for research funding. We created a strategic partnership focusing on urban social work. It was called URBAN SOS (urbansos. eu). The main goal was to reinvigorate the investigation of wider social and societal structures and the individualization of social problems while educating social work students and professionals in the field to be aware of, understand, analyze, and act on specific urban dimensions of social challenges and conflicts.

As Finland is a Nordic welfare state, and social work is a younger discipline here than in the United States, there has not been a great deal of focus on this work until recently. Recently, like elsewhere, Finland has become very much influenced by neoliberalism, as the welfare state concept is shrinking. Our third sector is growing, but there's very little discussion between frontline professionals and decision-makers about decisions that are being made to cut services and how that affects people practically. We believe bigger thinking is needed, and that is what the URBAN SOS project was all about.

Self-Care Tips

I read a lot of fun fiction that has nothing to do with social work! I enjoy traveling and listening to music. I live in Finland, the land of sauna, but I still enjoy a hot bath now and again. In Finland, spending time in the forest is also important. Even in the city here, there is a great deal of green space. Nature is part of self-care.

I also need to be aware of my boundaries—or lack thereof. One of the first research projects I did was about empathy. The research question was whether you could teach empathy to social work students. YES! We called the concept Qualified Empathy, and it's defined as the ability to reflectively and emotionally separate oneself from another and to understand the context; then in an intentional process, focus on understanding of the other person's viewpoint both cognitively and emotionally. Qualified Empathy means more supportive than reactive actions in client situations. This research process and the insights gained have helped me create stronger boundaries.

Practice Wisdom and Advice

- Follow your heart. Once you find your passion, the rewards will follow. Our MSW base degree gives us so many different skills and competencies that with a little fine-tuning or upskilling, our skills can be applied to many settings.
- Don't be surprised if the area that drew you in initially becomes less attractive at some point. No worries! Breathe... look around. Throw another scoop of water on the sauna rocks and wait for the steam to rise. Come up with a new plan and then act. Little steps are still steps. Go for what you want. There's a reason you want it. Find your passion, which is usually what is in your heart.

Final Thoughts

I believe everyone is valuable. Not every behavior is acceptable, but this doesn't take away from the human being behind the behavior. I also believe if we don't stand together, we'll fall apart. Compromise is difficult, but the other options are worse. Because Finland is a welfare state, with an attitude of communality, I have seen this philosophy in action, and it works!

I am profoundly grateful I moved from psychology to social work. Coming from the United States, I knew one way to see the world, social work, and social services. Moving to Finland was an eye-opener because I now view the world in a much different way. I became more aware of inequality all around me, and I recognize the many opportunities for social justice work. I don't blindly accept inequality. I became aware of power differentials and discriminatory practices. I am aware of my privilege and how it challenges me to look at where I can contribute to a more balanced distribution of power and knowledge. I believe everything happens for a reason, and as we only have one go-around, it's important to leave this place better than we found it.

Always a Social Worker

Christina C. Gigler, MSW, LCSW, ACSW

MSW: University of Maryland

BSW: Shippensburg University

Social Work Pathway and Work Experience

I grew up as a daughter of Ukrainian parents who immigrated to the United States from Poland two years before I was born. They went through a lot of hardship in their lives, but family, religion, and culture were strong and helped them survive. My grandmother lived with my family since I was three years old, which allowed both of my parents to work hard at several blue-collar jobs to help

Christina C. Gigler, MSW, LCSW, ACSW, presenting at her first national conference in Florida, 1996

provide us with many things they didn't have growing up in Poland. They instilled in me a strong work ethic, but I also saw how difficult it was to make it and the challenges my family persevered through. They wanted better for their kids and worked hard to make sure we had more than they did.

I was a first-generation college student and went to Shippensburg University for my undergraduate degree and began as a math major! As a freshman, I didn't get to pick my schedule. I had to take some general education courses, and I was fortunate to be put into an Intro to Social Work course. I had an incredible professor who was dynamic and opened my eyes to many of society's problems and issues. In that class, I realized that there were other people out there who also struggled. I wanted to help other people and help to be part of the change, so I changed my major to Social Work.

I wound up earning a BSW with a psychology minor. I had a strong field placement as a school social worker, engaged in volunteer work, and worked part-time in the social service field. But when I started applying for desired social work positions, they all required an MSW degree. So, I thought, *Why not? I have advanced standing credits, so I might as well go right to graduate school.*

I went to the University of Maryland at Baltimore. I began in the summer as a full-time student but struggled with managing school, work, and life. Fortunately, I had an incredible support person in my life in graduate school, who I joke was my "elevator buddy" because she set off the elevator alarm when I told her I was "quitting" graduate school and wouldn't stop it until I committed to staying in the program with her. I kept going and got my MSW that following May, so the advanced standing status paid off because I only had to go one full calendar year. My focus was administration and community organization.

As a field student, I wrote a grant, and for my first job post-MSW degree, I ended up being able to hire myself to complete quality assurance and program evaluation work for the Court Appointed Special Advocate (CASA) program in Baltimore, which I loved. We were working with volunteers who were working with youth stuck in the foster care system. It was an inspiring program that also provided me with strong mentorship and experiences.

I then moved to the Philadelphia area, where I worked for Catholic Social Services for almost two years. I recruited foster parents and completed home studies. I also had a caseload of children, working with them, their foster families, and their biological families. This was during the "crack baby" epidemic, so I was exposed to a lot of intense and medically fragile cases and ethical issues. During this time, I also used my grant-writing experience in volunteer capacities and worked with a group of individuals to develop the first CASA program in Delaware County, which still exists today.

I eventually moved back to the Lehigh Valley, Pennsylvania, and worked at KidsPeace for almost sixteen years in a variety of positions. My first job was a social worker on a unit with twenty male adolescents. Next, I became a clinical supervisor and managed one hundred youth in five houses, supervising eleven social workers. When I look back on my career, that was one of my favorite jobs. I love supervision, mentoring, and teaching. I dabbled in other jobs, and I went to the diagnostic program, worked in the training department, and worked in the psychiatric hospital in between maternity leaves of my now grown daughter and son. I was trying different things because I needed more flexibility for childcare reasons. I really got to know a lot about the mental health system, especially with youth and families. I also did some equine therapy work at a local equine farm working with adolescents with severe trauma issues. I remember, though, when I started doing more mental health work, especially the trauma cases, I had to get more training and completed some certificate programs. There is always so much to learn in this profession.

I naturally think about some of the cases, especially when I was in the diagnostic program. I worked with a lot of youth with suicidal ideation or attempted self-injury. There were a lot of traumas. When we would get a child in and I started working with them, I remember thinking, *There's no way we are going to be able to help this kid. This case is so complex, where do we even start?* But I loved working with the multidisciplinary team, including the psychiatrist, psychologist, nurses, counselors, and me as the social worker. We really got to know each kid, and I liked doing things outside of the box. If I couldn't reach a kid in talk therapy, we would do art therapy, play therapy, go for walks, runs, or play basketball. I started a small community garden right outside our building to get the youth out there, helping with the planting and weeding. Highlights were when I was able to see some kids who were our toughest cases start thriving. It was amazing to see their journey and know I had a part in that.

Because of my interest in clinical supervision, I led a training for social workers, and I had Dr. Phyllis Black in my class. We hit it off immediately. Then I started thinking, *I really want to do more teaching.* I was also having a difficult time working with adolescents while parenting two at home, so I knew it was time for a change. Eventually, I applied to two local MSW programs; each had a one-year temporary full-time faculty position. This was a huge leap for me.

I was offered both positions, and I accepted the job at Marywood, after being coaxed by Dr. Black. I cried my eyes out when I left KidsPeace because that program was in my heart. I worked at Marywood for almost sixteen years! First with three one-year appointments as a Clinical Instructor, then for nine years as a Field Director. I spent the rest of the time as Program Coordinator for the Lehigh Valley MSW program.

Since then, after a lot of life losses, I felt I needed a change again to allow me more flexibility and more time to pursue other interests. I realized how much I wanted to focus only on teaching and mentoring in what is, most likely, the last step in my professional social work career, *even if not the last on my life path as a social worker.* I now work at Widener University as a Clinical Assistant Professor. I am teaching on campus in Chester, Pennsylvania, as well as online. I find teaching very rewarding. I enjoy collaborating with students and agencies in diverse settings, many in the Philadelphia area. I appreciate working with students who are grasping for knowledge to learn how to help other people. When they start, their skills are raw, but by the end of the semester after learning and role playing, I can see the growth and confidence in them. I could not be prouder of my students and all they will do to help others. I love sharing my mistakes and wisdom with students as I work to pass on the torch to the next generation of social workers.

Self-Care Tips

The one thing I want to highlight is the importance of self-care, because burnout can be part of the profession. It took a long time for me to realize the work that we do is important, but it's so taxing that it's okay to say, "I need some time for me."

It's also okay to not work all of the time. We need to stand up for ourselves and be comfortable being a voice for ourselves as we are for others. We need to be a leader at the different tables we work around, not just part of the discussion, and not just accept things as they are or accept the unreasonable work demands placed on us. This can be difficult at times, but it's critical if we wish to have long careers in this profession and stay healthy and effective.

Self-care for me is a work in progress. I have a lot of hobbies and enjoy reading, baking, cooking, gardening, and photography. This summer I was not working, so I did a lot of traveling, and I thrive on that. Fortunately, my husband loves traveling too. I love exploring the world, seeing new cultures, meeting new people, and seeing how other people do things. I love that I can bring those experiences to all parts of my life. With each trip, I learn to cook differently, live a little better, and even teach differently.

I walk every day. I love walking my dog, but I'm also addicted to my Fitbit. I must get in at least my 10,000 steps in a day. I love being outdoors, and I'm happiest in the mountains or at the beach. I hike, bike, backpack, and kayak, and I bought a paddle board this summer, which has been fun to try. In the winter, I like to cross-country ski and hike with my ice spikes. I like any kind of adventure activity. Being out in nature is definitely something I need to do every day. It is part of my self-care, but also part of my mindfulness and spiritual practice, and it also helps me keep going as a social worker.

Practice Wisdom and Advice

- If you ever feel you're stuck in your career, try something else! Think out of the box. There are many positions in so many different fields of social work. One of the things I love about the profession is that you could do macro work. You could do micro work. You could work with communities or individuals, find something else, mix it up. Volunteer in your community. I think it's healthy to mix things up. We get stagnant if we stay in the same place too long. Each time I changed jobs in my career, it allowed me to grow. My advice would be to find something different. Don't let yourself just be stuck and comfortable. Sometimes we create our own roadblocks, preventing us from moving forward. Take that leap, try something new.

Christina C. Gigler, MSW, LCSW, ACSW, with Phyllis Black, PhD, MSW, ACSW, at Marywood School of Social Work

- Get involved in our professional organization. My values mirror the values in the NASW Code of Ethics, and I have used them to guide me throughout my career. I have been a member of NASW since I was an undergrad student, and I have not let my membership lapse. I even served as a BSW student board representative. Being a member of NASW is worth every penny because I don't think our profession would be where it is today if we didn't have a national association advocating for us and making sure we have continuing education. I have held various leadership positions in my local division, including Eastern Division Chair, and NASW-PA board member for three years. Currently, I'm on the Ethics Committee for Pennsylvania, which I really enjoy.
- Get involved in your community and networks. Volunteer to be on boards and in groups. I currently am involved with Resilient Lehigh Valley, a trauma awareness collaborative through the United Way of the Greater Lehigh Valley. It is rewarding to work with a variety of social workers, educators, and leaders in our community. I also have been working with the Emmaus High School Angel Network in my local community, assisting students and families in need to help them be successful in school. Social work skills have such a great application to do many good things that can also energize us while helping others.

- Value supervision. I don't think I'd be where I am today if I didn't have good supervision along the way. A critical part of social work practice is to find that person or people to do clinical supervision throughout your career. Look for mentors to guide you. I am fortunate to have had mentors such as Phyllis Black, Hope Horowitz, Krista Strantz, Karen Rogers, Michelle Brandt, and many others along the way.

Final Thoughts

Because I am not very patient, it is challenging for me to deal with all types of bureaucracy. But, as a social worker, I try very hard to navigate that and I do not take "no" easily. I always try to find a way to either meet in the middle or try to get people to see other sides of things. I like the challenge, even though I find it very frustrating sometimes. I wonder what it's going to take to make a change happen. How are we going to fix this system that is so broken and not working anymore? Advocacy is such a big part of social work, whether working with clients, students, or our communities. I enjoy working to empower others and trying to figure out a way to help somebody.

I like to joke that no matter where I am, somehow people know I'm a social worker. No matter what I'm wearing, it's on me—even if I'm in the grocery store, people start telling me their problems! It's just who I am. I'm the oldest in my family of four, so I was always the natural helper, the natural leader. I still am. If my friends or family needs something, they know they can call me, and I usually know how to help them or I will find the resources to do so.

What guides me every day is that I want to be a good person. Every day, I ask myself, *How am I going to be a good person today? What can I do to help other people? To make this a better world?* Be good, be kind, be helpful: That is my life's purpose.

My Journey as a Social Worker: A Wonderful Ride

Phyllis Black, PhD, MSW, ACSW

PhD: National Catholic School of Social Service (NCSSS)

MSW: McGill University

BA: McGill University

Social Work Pathway and Work Experience

Prescience: I grew up in Montreal, Québec, Canada, a short bike ride from the Université de Montréal, which I often visited. On one such visit in June, it happened to be the day of the University's commencement. I was smitten by the pomp and circumstance and especially loved what I called the "costumes of the teachers"—the academic regalia of the faculty. Captivated by their uniforms, I

In "costume"

decided that when I grew up, I was going to be a professor.

    College and Pathway to Social Work: Fast-forward to my college days, when I pursued both my undergraduate (BA) and graduate studies (MSW) at McGill University. During my undergraduate years, I enrolled in several sociology and economics courses, which proved to be eye-opening. Coming from a privileged background, I was deeply affected by learning about the extent of social injustice in our society and the prevalence of structural and institutional inequity. I decided, *bag the costume* and instead committed myself to promoting social justice and improving the lives of marginalized and oppressed individuals.

When I completed my undergraduate degree with a dual major in sociology and psychology, I discussed my future career path with my parents. I told them, "I think I want to be a lawyer." I viewed entering this profession *as a means of realizing my commitment to social justice. I envisioned myself advocating for people unable to navigate the complexity and expense of the legal system. I believed that this was how I could make a difference in terms of advancing justice. This conversation took place in the late 1950s. My parents' response was, "No. Women can't be lawyers. It's a male's profession. Here are your options. You can either be a teacher, a nurse, or a social worker."* Given my aversion to blood and gore, nursing was ruled out. Teaching held some appeal, but having enjoyed my experiences as a camp counselor and most recently as head counselor, I felt a tug toward social work. Thus, my choice of a career in social work was launched.

MSW Studies: I thoroughly enjoyed my time in the MSW program. It validated my choice of social work as a career. I was learning how to make a difference in the lives of people. The dual focus of the profession on individual well-being and social advocacy aligned with my interest in social justice. The school allowed me to cobble together a unique study plan that combined working with individuals and groups. I came to love group work.

First Jobs: Like most Montrealers, I lived at home while attending McGill. After completing my MSW, I felt it was time to leave the nest and spread my wings. With two friends, we decided that New York was the place to go, and we made the move to Manhattan. With social justice in my mind, I took a job in East Harlem working with street gangs. In fact, it was in the same neighborhood where *West Side Story* was filmed. Just as in the film, there were ongoing turf battles—rumbles— between the Puerto Rican youths, who were the newcomers, and the African American youths, who grew up there. Both gangs had knives and guns. Our mission, as gang workers, was to intervene in these fights in an effort to reduce the frequent injuries and occasional deaths. Our strategy was to provide social and athletic opportunities for these young people to ease their hostilities. Tragically, we never quite accomplished our mission during my time there.

Growing up in Montreal there was minimal cultural diversity. My three-year stint in Harlem was a major life-changing experience. In preparation for the job, I had read everything I could about diversity and poverty. Nonetheless, arriving on the scene was a profound culture shock. The neighborhood was in chaos, with shuttered storefronts, giant rats everywhere, frequent house fires, and the unforgettable yucky feeling of cockroaches crawling up my legs while visiting clients' houses. This was my introduction to the remarkable phenomenon of having my clients serve as my mentors. This phenomenon has continued throughout my career whereby clients, students, and colleagues have provided valuable insights that deeply shaped my journey as a social worker. It was incredibly impactful to experience firsthand the devastating effects of poverty, racism, and marginalization. Furthermore, I left Montreal with delusions of grandeur, believing that I would change the world and make a humongous difference. I quickly got a lesson in humility. I learned that even making a difference in the lives of one or two kids represented an accomplishment. For these reasons and more, I highlight this job as one of my most impactful and transformational. To this day, I'm so grateful for this experience.

My roommates and I lived in midtown Manhattan. I drove to work in a small, red convertible. The car was light, and the kids delighted in lifting it up and moving it to different spots and watching me search for it. Although the streets of Harlem were perilous, the kids protected me as I walked at night looking for my car.

During that time, I was dating Perry, who would become my husband. One night, he came to visit me in Harlem. There was a rumble, and he saw me in the middle of the angry crowd, shouting, "Get out! Get out! Leave. The cops are coming!"

"Who the *$%# called the cops?" the kids asked.

"I did because I'm going to do everything possible to keep you safe," I said.

The kids scattered, and the cops came. I felt gratified, but it made Perry very anxious. Upon getting in the car, out of nowhere a throng of kids emerged, lifted the car, and shook it. When the kids finally put the car down, Perry said, "I have to get you out of here. Let's get married."

At the time, he was a neurosurgery resident at Johns Hopkins University Hospital, so off I went to Baltimore. I well remember the day I left Harlem. I wept because I had become attached to the kids. I had hope for the future for two of them, but I had no idea what would happen to most of the others. I wasn't very optimistic.

Hopkins: My first job as a social worker at Johns Hopkins was in the Department of Psychiatry. There I met Virginia Satir, a social work icon, who gave a talk on family therapy using family sculpture techniques and other experiential approaches. While the McGill School of Social Work curriculum had a psychodynamic orientation, Virginia Satir favored a humanistic, client-centered engagement approach. She thereby gave me permission to break away from the stilted psychoanalytic method, as well as the flexibility to use interventions that I perceived to be in the best interests of my clients. This was another pivotal experience and became a guiding theme for all my subsequent work.

The Director of the Department of Social Work recognized my enthusiasm for working with groups. She charged me with identifying possible needs around the hospital for group services. This was a dream assignment, and I eagerly got right on it. I started a group for partners of patients with laryngeal cancer; a group for little people (persons with dwarfism); several ongoing groups for significant others in surgical waiting rooms; and an activity group for children with anger control issues. Two of these groups are particularly memorable. In the Department of Psychiatry, I worked with a group of parents whose children were being treated for behavioral health problems. My inclination at the time was to advocate a simplistic approach: *All you have to do is love your children unconditionally and set reasonable disciplinary boundaries, and they will grow up to become upstanding citizens.* Then I had my own children and realized that parenting is among the most rewarding but also the most challenging responsibilities in the world. There is no formulaic, one-size-fits-all recipe. The parents in that program added to my list of client mentors. They knocked the smugness out of me and underscored the importance of humility.

Another group that stands out in my memory was on a pediatric ward. This was a group of young teenagers with terminal diseases. There were two policies at Hopkins at the time. First, the children were not to be told when a fellow patient died. Instead, they were told the patient was sent to the fourteenth floor. Second, the children themselves were not to be told their diagnosis nor prognosis.

At the first group session, we set the objectives and ground rules for the conduct of the group. About ten minutes before the second group session, "Sam," one of the teens on the ward, died. He died with a football on his bed falsely suggesting the optimistic belief that he would recover in time to play his favorite sport. During that period, I was avidly reading the pioneering scholarship of Elizabeth Kübler-Ross on death and dying, from which I derived many insights. I was certain that the teens understood what "went to the fourteenth floor" meant. I was certain that they knew it was a euphemism for death. The "don't tell" policy deprived them of mourning a ward mate. Furthermore, the policy regarding withholding their diagnosis and prognosis, which I felt they already knew, deprived them of the opportunity of talking about their condition, their hopes, and their fears with family, friends, and hospital staff. As well, it precluded their participation in determining their treatment plans.

When I went into the group meeting, the first question they asked me was, "Where's 'Sam'?" I thought, *Yikes, I am in the throes of an ethical dilemma. Do I follow hospital policy, or do I have a categorical imperative to act on what I think is in the best interest of my clients?* This dilemma, incidentally, further fueled my sustained interest in ethical issues in social work. Taken aback, I said something pretty inept like, "Where do you think 'Sam' is?" Their response: "Cut the *$%$. Just tell us where 'Sam' is." I plopped down on the side of telling them, doing so at the risk of violating hospital policy, because I felt they already knew. I took a deep breath and revealed that "Sam" had died. After a period of silence, one of the teens spoke up: "I have the same disease as Sam. I think I may be next." That began a profound discussion about their fears of death and loss, which continued for many group sessions. Fortunately, the discussions resulted in favorable outcomes. With my encouragement and some role playing, the teens were able to talk openly with their parents and hospital personnel about their disease and fears. Equally gratifying was that together the group members and I were able to impact both existing hospital policies. In addition to our advocacy, I arranged for Elizabeth Kübler-Ross to speak at pediatric grand rounds. Her compelling presentation served as the main catalyst for policy change. The group expressed their gratitude to me by gifting me a pair of earrings, donated by one of their parents, which they called "hearings" in recognition of my willingness to listen to their fears and anguish. To this day, I treasure these "hearings" as precious mementos.

This group also became my mentors. They taught me to stay in the tunnel of their angst. One touching thought that remains is that they were less concerned about their own death and more about how their parents would cope with losing them. Another crucial insight was the realization of the power of advocacy in changing social policy. As my children were growing, I began to see their faces in the faces of the children who were dying. Yet another takeaway: There are life circumstances that suggest maybe this is not the time for this type of work. It's time for me to move on and turn the group over to another social worker.

While in New York, I accepted an invitation to deliver a guest lecture at Columbia University School of Social Work on my work in Harlem. My many hours of preparation far exceeded the one-hour allotted lecture time and introduced me to the demanding nature of teaching. The experience was gratifying and intriguing. Later, while at Hopkins, when I was asked to teach a course in group work at the University of Maryland, I jumped at the opportunity. This fueled my tendency to stretch myself and operate out of my comfort zone—a tendency that persists to this very day. I taught for several semesters, and I became hooked on becoming an academic. I especially enjoyed seeing the "aha" moment on the faces of the students when they finally grasped a complex concept. Pursuing a doctorate in social work seemed the appropriate next step. The only convenient option at that time was The Catholic University's National Catholic School of Social Service (NCSSS) in Washington, DC. I decided to test the waters as a part-time non-matriculating student. After a successful semester, I felt, *Okay, I think I can do this* and went on to officially apply for admission. I was rejected. The letter said: "She is the wife of a neurosurgeon, and the mother of three young children. We hesitate to invest in her education as we believe she will not make a significant contribution to the social work profession." I appealed the rejection to the eminent social work educator Dean Dorothy Daily, who read the letter, tore it up, and said, "Welcome to the doctoral program!" It was a moment I will never forget. I thought about that letter and its message when, several years later, I received an Outstanding Alumni award from the program for my contributions to social work. And yes, I did get to wear the "costume" at graduation and for many years thereafter.

Marywood: Following graduation from NCSSS, I accepted a position in the MSW program as a part-time instructor, with my expectation of continuing in this role for at least a while. However, fate intervened when my husband was offered a job as Chief of Neurosurgery in Philadelphia, prompting our relocation from Baltimore, and uprooting my plans. The move was disorienting for me and especially for my teenaged children. After a frantic period of trying to settle our family into our new surroundings, I was ready to begin a search for work. At the time, there were several MSW programs in the area.

Despite feeling tempted to apply to the more prestigious programs in the area, Marywood University proved a good fit for me. Fortunately, I had numerous opportunities to guest lecture at the other schools, which helped me overcome any remaining temptations. While Marywood encouraged scholarship, it prioritized teaching over a militant "publish or perish" mandate. Being freed from the pressure to constantly produce scholarship allowed me to conduct research and to publish on my own time schedule. My main areas of scholarship included ethical issues in social work and topics related to social work education.

I am indebted to the support and mentorship of Dr. Terry Singer, a gifted Dean at Marywood School of Social Work. He nudged me to become active in the National Association of Social Workers (NASW) and the Council of Social Work Education (CSWE). My association with these organizations provided invaluable learning opportunities. I had the privilege to interact with some of the "movers and shakers" in the field, and I profited from their wisdom and expertise. They too were my mentors.

CSWE: My time at CSWE was particularly meaningful. I was a volunteer at the organization for more than 20 years, participating on various committees, conducting accreditation visits, and serving as a member of the Board of Directors. My most daunting and ultimately most rewarding challenge was my role as Chair of the Commission on Curriculum and Educational Innovation. Once again, "I'm 'in over my head.'"

Fortunately, it was the commissioners who provided the ideas. My task was simply to keep things moving along, which I was somehow able to do, relying heavily on my group work training. After five years of intensive work, the Commission produced a document that revitalized the future of social work education by shifting the structure of pedagogy from a content-based to a competency-based framework. Programs were freed to design curricula that met a set of competencies, launching the opportunity for innovation.

Teaching Evolution: As a neophyte professor, I felt compelled to teach students everything I knew about the subject. My presentations were packed with facts. A number of influences steered me away from this philosophy and led me down several other pathways. I came upon a disquieting study suggesting that by the time a student reaches the doorknob of the classroom, 60 percent of the content presented is gone. The loss escalates exponentially over time.

This study was an eye-opener and prompted me to explore other ways of teaching. My first "other way" was to identify three central concepts that I wanted students to take away from the class, and to laser focus on these concepts. My rationale was that if they grasped these concepts, additional details could be readily accessed from other resources. Furthermore, most influential in my teaching evolution was observing the approach of colleagues, notably Professor Hope Horowitz. Her creative use of experiential, hands-on activities both engaged students and enhanced their understanding of the material. In yet another "teaching turnaround," I began to integrate experiential learning into my research and ethics classes. Research was a real challenge. Students were resistant to this course, which they (erroneously) judged to be irrelevant to social work practice. I used a *Jeopardy!* template as well as other similar interactive techniques to enhance participation and relevancy.

In teaching ethics, I presented authentic case examples for class deliberation, which enriched student involvement and fostered their learning of ethical-decision-making resolution. I used a series of props and role-play scenarios to address ethical boundary challenges. For example: Assuming the role of a grateful client, I would offer the students, who were acting as my social workers, a tin of cookies. The students would then debate whether it was ethical to accept the cookies and the implications of their varying decisions. I would continue ratcheting up the scenarios, including offering a wrapped gift, and a hug for receiving a GED. Based on these deliberations, the students would collectively develop a set of guidelines to address professional boundary maintenance.

I have loved teaching, and I am deeply thankful to my students and colleagues for their ongoing mentorship. I often think that I have learned more than I have taught.

Wonderful ride!: I made the right choice in choosing social work as my career. It has been a challenging and thoroughly fulfilling journey. Although I am retired from academia, I continue to dabble in the field, presenting webinars and guest lectures, and doing consulting work for social work education programs on curriculum design. In addition, serving on the MA NASW Committee on Ethics allows me to maintain my long-standing interest in ethics. It's truly been a wonderful ride!

Final Thoughts

This is social work's time. There is widespread recognition that our profession can contribute to addressing the social and economic problems currently facing our nation and the world. Our dual mission to individual well-being and social justice is uniquely valuable for these turbulent times. We honor the legacy of our past historical heroes who have spearheaded major social advances in our society. We stand on the shoulders of such giants as Jane Addams, Mary Richmond, Ida Wells, Francis Perkins, Whitney Young, and Dorothy Height. Now it's our turn to seed our legacy so that tomorrow's social workers can stand on our shoulders.

- Be brave
- Be bold
- Be badass—engage in "good trouble"
- Let your voices be heard
- Be nimble: Embrace challenge and change in the certainty of uncertain times
- Value the work that you do
- Champion social progress

With my best wishes, onward!

Accepting CSWE Leadership Award   Scooting down the halls at Marywood   Presenting at an NASW Conference

A Career Based on Social Action

Hope Horowitz, MSW, LSW

MSW: University of Michigan

BA: Sociology, Ithaca College

Social Work Pathway and Work Experience

I always thought I wanted to be a language teacher. In high school, I enjoyed learning Spanish and French, and so began as a Spanish major in college. Advisors suggested combining business and Spanish, but I knew that was not for me. I also did not get good grades in the Spanish courses, so I needed a new direction.

I went to career services and took assessment tests to help me determine a new path. The results pointed me toward social services. Once I started taking sociology and psychology courses, I had my new direction. I also spent a semester during my junior year at Ithaca College in London. That experience opened my eyes to new cultures and travel.

Upon graduating with a degree in sociology, I applied to more than one hundred jobs—and did not get one interview! I knew I needed to take a different route.

JFK's quote, "Ask not what your country can do for you, ask what you can do for your country," led me to become a Volunteers in Service to America (VISTA) volunteer. Today, VISTA is known as AmeriCorps VISTA. The purpose of the program was to serve a community in need to build capacity and live on the economic level of the people being served. This was a powerful experience for me. I was placed in Atlanta, Georgia, (quite different from New York where I am from) and worked at a youth development center setting up a volunteer mentor program for adjudicated youth. This was a difficult placement because I was unsure if what we were doing would really help change the trajectory of the lives of those at the center. I also volunteered for B'nai B'rith Youth Organization (BBYO), a Jewish youth group for adolescents, as an advisor for a chapter in Atlanta where the focus was on leadership development. This helped me balance and believe what I was doing was helpful. On one hand, I was organizing volunteers to serve as mentors for the youth in detention and on the other hand I was helping teens develop their identity and leadership skills.

At the end of my VISTA service, I was asked to staff BBYO's three-week leadership training camp in the Pocono Mountains of Pennsylvania, which sounded like a good idea because I still did not have a job! The leadership training camp attracted top teen leaders from around the world. As a leadership staff member at the age of twenty-two, I taught the leadership curriculum and learned how to deal with life issues teens faced. Two teens in my bunk were child abuse cases. The director of the camp was a PhD/MSW and guided me to know how to handle these intense situations. That was an eye-opening experience for me.

When the camp program concluded, I was offered my choice of a job as Program Director for Michigan Region BBYO or a position back in Atlanta. I could not decide what to do, so I asked for advice. I was told the Director in Michigan would provide excellent supervision, and that made my decision. This was my first actual job! I loved the work I did guiding teens and developing programs and conventions. Arnie Weiner, MSW, the Michigan Regional Director, was my mentor. (He is also featured in this book!) He taught me how to work

Hope Horowitz, MSW, LSW, at her first job with Michigan Region BBYO

with teens and guided me on how to develop strong programs, run an office, create budgets, and more. Our weekly supervision built my confidence. I loved what I was doing, but after two years, I received a letter saying my position was retrenched.

BBYO offered me a scholarship to get an MSW because they wanted me to stay with the agency and advance. In exchange, I would work for BBYO upon graduation. BBYO preferred I attend Wayne State University in Detroit with a focus on group work. I applied to both Wayne State and the University of Michigan. I did not get accepted to Wayne State, but I was accepted at the University of Michigan, which was the top social work school in the country! I learned a valuable lesson: Always reach for things that might appear out of reach. I never understood

Hope Horowitz, MSW, LSW, with Arnie Weiner, MSW, at a dinner honoring Arnie in 2023

how I got accepted to U of M, but not Wayne State! I attended the University of Michigan with a focus on community organization.

Upon graduating with my MSW, I was offered a job as the Regional Director for Central Region East BBYO with offices in Allentown, Pennsylvania. The region served more than 500 teens and twelve communities in eastern Pennsylvania and Delaware. At the time, things were more patriarchal. While I wanted that position, the agency was concerned that a young woman like me would be traveling to visit these communities by myself. This motivated me even more to take the job!

I had met my husband in Michigan on a blind date. One of the BBYO volunteer advisors introduced us, and we were married one year before moving to Allentown, Pennsylvania. We thought we would stay for two years so I could fulfill my commitment for receiving the scholarship. I wound up working for Central Region East BBYO for fourteen years. During that time, I led a six-week teen trip to Israel, led and developed programs for weekend conventions serving up to 250 teens, and built a strong region to help teens develop their leadership skills, self-confidence, and identity. I spent most summers teaching leadership at the camp in the Poconos, and I enjoyed the experiential learning and ability to develop relationships with teens and staff. I loved being Regional Director, and it was hard to leave the job. But, after fourteen years, it was time for a change.

I was offered a job at the Allentown Jewish Community Center and served as their Assistant Director for nine years. In all the jobs I held, my favorite part was always the training aspects. While training was not formal teaching, I loved experiential learning and the teaching parts of each job.

After twenty-three years of agency work, I decided I wanted to be out of administration and teach at the college level. While I always loved administrative roles, I was ready to leave behind the politics that administrators deal with in these roles. In addition to working at the JCC, I was an adjunct instructor for Marywood University's MSW program in the Lehigh Valley and taught courses at the community college. After leaving the JCC, I spent the next year teaching BSW and MSW students full-time at Kutztown University of Pennsylvania and the following year teaching MSW students at Marywood part-time while developing a social work continuing education business.

Then a full-time social work faculty position opened at Northampton Community College (NCC) in Bethlehem, Pennsylvania. I applied, and the rest is history! I began teaching at NCC in 2007 and continue to serve as the Social Work Program Coordinator. I teach social work and sociology courses both on campus and online.

My passion is being involved in social justice issues. The most powerful experiences I have had at NCC have been traveling with students. I planned and co-led seven trips to help rebuild in the Lower Ninth Ward in New Orleans after Hurricane Katrina. But before that I worked on several projects to help those affected by Katrina. The first project I was involved with was helping to organize a prom dress drive to bring dresses to girls in Ocean Springs and Biloxi, Mississippi. The BSW students in the group work course I was teaching helped organize the dresses, fundraise, and publicize the collection. One student went with a small group from the Lehigh Valley to deliver more than 2,200 dresses! The following year, students in my MSW administration class designed a project they called "Box of Hope." They collected items for starter kits for people moving into Federal Emergency Management Agency (FEMA) trailers, organized them, and delivered them to Coventry House in New Orleans for distribution. Starter kits provided people with basics needed to get a home started, such as towels, sheets, dishes, pots and pans, etc.

Hope Horowitz, MSW, LSW, helping rebuild in New Orleans

Most powerful for me was helping to rebuild homes in the Lower Ninth Ward of New Orleans. It was life-altering. Seeing the devastation of homes wiped away from the breach of the levees and inequity firsthand required me to learn as much as I could about what happened and why and then share that information with students. To this day, these seven trips were some of the most impactful experiences I have had as a social worker.

Additional trips included taking students to Ecuador, Israel, and most recently Finland. My colleagues and I developed a Mindful Travel Mentors trip to Finland for social work students, faculty, and professionals. These trips enabled me to develop relationships with social workers internationally. I continue to work on social work projects with colleagues abroad.

Hope at an NASW Continuing Ed workshop

Because service is an important social work value, I was involved with our local National Association of Social Workers

(NASW) Division. I served in various leadership roles, including three years as Eastern Division Chair. I have also presented at numerous conferences over the years.

When I look in the rearview mirror of my career, the puzzle pieces seem to come together. I recognized that I was always a teacher, either informally or formally, whether it was working with teens developing leadership programs, leading staff trainings, or teaching social work continuing education workshops or formal college teaching. It is now evident how the various parts of my career unfolded. I also recognize my love of culture and travel was inspired by the semester I spent in London as a student at Ithaca College. In the beginning of my story, I said I wanted to be a teacher, but that was not the direction I wound up taking initially. However, it is what I have been doing for most of my career. Somehow, I knew as a teenager that teaching was my ultimate passion.

Social work provides me with a way to live a life with values important to me and to advocate and stand up for justice. Social work incorporates the personal and professional values that I live by. Finding a profession that coincides with one's personal philosophy of life is a gift.

Self-Care Tips

The year I was a VISTA volunteer, I learned to meditate. At the time, transcendental meditation was popular, and that is the method I learned. I have been meditating for more than forty-five years! Meditating keeps me grounded.

Hope's VISTA certificate

I also practice yoga and enjoy walks, traveling, puzzles, listening to audiobooks, and spending time with family and friends. I also value sleep a great deal!

Practice Wisdom and Advice

- Find a mentor(s), someone you can look up to, who will take time to guide you and be there for you whenever needed.
- Find good supervision and take advantage of a good supervisor's knowledge and skill.
- Find supportive colleagues because it is important to have people to talk to whom you can trust and who understand your world.

Hope Horowitz, MSW, LSW, with her family (from left, son Jason, Hope, godson Josh, daughter Rachel, and husband Stuart) at an NASW Conference in 2016, where Hope received a Lifetime Achievement Award

- When someone says "no" to something you want to do and believe in, don't take "no" for an answer! Find a way to follow your passion… there is always a way with persistence.
- Recognize and take advantage of opportunities that present themselves. Don't make excuses to remain in your comfort zone.
- If you are not happy in a job, *leave!*
- Always continue to learn, grow, and experience new things.
- We are all global citizens. Take advantage of travel opportunities that come your way and learn about other cultures and ways of life.
- Don't be afraid to ask questions.
- Use random reach outs to other social workers to develop long-term relationships locally, nationally, and globally.
- Remember it is okay to try something that ends up not working! We all learn from mistakes. They are usually gifts in disguise!
- Have a positive attitude and maintain a sense of humor.

Final Thoughts

Something that remains with me to this day is when I graduated from Ithaca College, we were given a postcard with four simple lines from the poem ITHAKA by C.P. Cavafy. The lines chosen were:

> "Keep Ithaka always in mind.
> Arriving there is what you are destined for.
> But don't hurry the journey at all.
> Better if it goes on for years."

This poem reminds me how arrivals create change in our lives. It is the path and process in between that provide us with new challenges, opportunities, and choices. Try not to rush the process and take time to enjoy the adventures on your social work journey.

Interdisciplinary Teams and Working with Colleagues

Reading through the stories, I expect you noticed the importance of social workers being part of interdisciplinary teams in a variety of settings. Learning from different professionals and their viewpoints helps us provide the best resources possible to those we serve.

Equally important is finding colleagues you support and who will support you because it elevates what can be accomplished. Ideas can be shared and put into action as a team. I have been fortunate to have wonderful colleagues throughout my career. I would like to recognize two colleagues I worked closely with since I began teaching at Northampton Community College in Bethlehem, Pennsylvania, in 2007. These colleagues have degrees in sociology and communication. Combining our energies, viewpoints, and ideas enabled us to create some exciting experiences for students, faculty, and social work professionals.

Erin Reilly in New Orleans

Erin Reilly is a sociology professor at Northampton Community College. Erin earned her MA in Sociology from Lehigh University in Bethlehem, Pennsylvania. She has been teaching at NCC for over twenty years and held various leadership positions in the sociology department. She is passionate about taking trips with students and has led trips to New Orleans, Ecuador, Turkey, and Finland. She has also traveled to Japan through a Community College for International Development program. Erin has presented at numerous conferences nationally and internationally.

Erin and I have been "partners" since our first trip in 2009 when we took students to volunteer and help rebuild in the Lower Ninth Ward of New Orleans after Hurricane Katrina. In total, we co-led seven trips to NOLA between 2009 and 2012. These trips were powerful experiences for both of us and all participants as we saw the devastation from Hurricane Katrina firsthand. We helped rebuild homes and a community center, and cleaned flood-damaged lots and properties in the Lower Ninth Ward. Some may wonder if volunteering is worth it. The answer is YES! We worked with five organizations and had seventy-two student participants who provided 2,340 hours of volunteer service. Our motto was "Be the Change" and we were!

Erin and Hope in New Orleans

Erin and Hope having a lunch break in Lower Ninth Ward

Hope and Erin rebuilding

Erin and Hope outside a home where we helped with mold remediation

Our next adventure with students was co-leading a service trip to Ecuador. The trip was a cultural wonder as we stayed in Pimampiro, Ecuador, in the beautiful Andes Mountains. We spent time volunteering with an elementary school, senior center, and a summer camp operated by Peace Corps volunteers.

We were fortunate to explore the area and the culture of the Quechua people whose home is in the Andes Mountains.

Erin and I realized we have taken fourteen trips together over the years!

Erin and Hope hiking in the Andes Mountains, Ecuador

Hope and Erin in the Andes Mountains, Ecuador

Indigenous Quechua traveling in the Andes Mountains

Indigenous Quechua preparing for a ceremony in the Andes Mountains

Donna Acerra is a communication professor at Northampton Community College. She earned an MA in Communication at Temple University in Philadelphia, Pennsylvania. She has been teaching at NCC since 1989 and co-founded the Communication Studies program (AA). Donna has led student exchanges and study abroad experiences since 2008 with institutional partners in France, Costa Rica, and the Navajo Reservation. Donna created a course in 2010 with Dr. Miranda Haskie, a sociology professor at Diné College, Tsaile, Arizona, which led to cultural exchanges between students at both colleges over a five-year period. Students spent time with host families learning about the values, beliefs, and practices of each other's cultures. Donna has been the recipient of

Miranda Haskie and Donna Acerra in the Canyon de Chelly

several prestigious awards given to exemplary NCC faculty. Off campus, she is a founding member of "Luminaria Night," an annual city-wide celebration of community and giving, involving hundreds of volunteers working together to provide for neighbors in need in Bethlehem, Pennsylvania.

Due to our passion for travel, Donna, Erin, and I decided to put our ideas together during the 2016 fall semester. We created the "Mindful Travel" model. The goal was for the "teacher to become the learner" through a transformative and educational global experience. We asked other faculty to come with us and decided to go to Finland since Donna had family there and they could assist us. The faculty trip occurred at the end of the spring 2017 semester. To prepare, each participant was asked to "randomly reach out" to others in their discipline and make connections so we could learn about the differences in our educational and social service systems. I reached out to the International Federation of Social Workers and connected with Leigh Anne Rauhala (see her story on page 114). We developed a partnership between NCC and Metropolia University of Applied Sciences in Helsinki and continue to work together!

Intentional and mindful processing was used daily to help us stay focused in the moment and experience. Ideas were stimulated and our global awareness expanded. We each brought new ideas from the trip back to our classrooms, helping replace assumptions with cultural understanding, empathy, and new insights for problem solving. The connections we made with educators and professionals continue to generate global friendships and partnerships. It felt like a "mini sabbatical"!

In the fall of 2018, Donna, Erin, and I presented at the NASW PA conference about the difference in the Finnish educational and welfare systems and why Finland continues to be the happiest country in the world. There was great interest from participants to go to Finland with us. After the conference, we brainstormed and developed the "Mindful Travel Mentors" trip to Finland. The purpose was to provide a transformative, global learning experience for social work traditional and non-traditional students, faculty, and professionals. One of the goals of this immersive intercultural experience was to develop mentor relationships among the participants as well as with our Finnish partners. Traveling together as a group provided a unique networking opportunity for students to create relationships and connections with social work professionals, faculty, and other students. Reflection tools were used as a means for self-discovery and developing cultural competencies. Mentorships and global partnerships developed organically among participants.

Working *with my colleagues* was the key to developing these innovative, exciting experiences. It is important to remember the power of working with colleagues and interdisciplinary teams. Connect with others and build your network!

Erin, Hope, and Donna at a conference in Finland

Erin, Donna, and Hope in Finland

My Social Work Path
Questions to Ponder

I hope you have been inspired by the stories you read and the possibilities a career in social work offers. You have probably done some self-reflection about your own journey and where you are headed with your social work career as you read other people's stories. Maybe you are working on your degree, new in the profession, looking for a change in your area of practice, or a seasoned social worker.

Mindful, purposeful reflection helps us to review what is important in our lives and determine where we are headed. On the following pages, you will find a series of questions that will challenge you to think about yourself and what it means to be a social worker. How will you write YOUR story?

What made you pick social work as your career?

_____
_____
_____
_____
_____

What are your top three to five values that guide your life and work?

_____
_____
_____
_____
_____
_____

What do you do for self-care?

_____
_____
_____
_____

What are your strengths?

_____
_____
_____
_____

What are your challenges?

_____
_____
_____
_____
_____

Hope Horowitz, MSW, LSW

What are you grateful for?

_____
_____
_____
_____
_____

What is your life philosophy that guides you as a social worker?

_____
_____
_____
_____
_____

Who is your social work mentor?

_____
_____
_____
_____
_____

Where do you see yourself in the next 3, 5, 10, 20, 30+ years?

_____
_____
_____
_____
_____

What wisdom can you offer to others from your experience?

_____
_____
_____
_____

What else are you thinking about that will help create YOUR story?

_____
_____
_____
_____
_____

Acknowledgments

To Northampton Community College, Bethlehem, Pennsylvania, for supporting my endeavors over the years.

To My Mentors

Dr. Jules Burgevin, Ithaca College Sociology Professor, who taught me self-awareness and self-reflection.

Dr. Lew Hamburger, B'nai B'rith Youth Organization Leadership Camps, who took me under his wing and taught me how to deal with difficult situations using empathy and compassion.

Arnie Weiner, MSW, Michigan Region B'nai B'rith Youth Organization, who taught me how to be a professional, including leading an organization, administrative skills, how to work with adolescents, and the importance of community involvement.

Dr. Phyllis Black, Professor Emerita and retired Director of the Marywood University Lehigh Valley MSW Program, who is a mentor and role model to me and thousands of social workers and students. She continues to teach us the importance of being ethical in our work.

To the thousands of **students** I have been honored to teach over the years. You have each inspired me and taught me valuable life lessons.

To My Family

My husband, **Stuart,** also a social worker, who spent his career as a psychotherapist. My career was spent in administration and teaching, representing the versatility of the social work profession. Social work values continue to permeate our relationship and family values. I appreciate his undying love and support for my work over the years.

My children, **Jason and Rachel,** for their continued support and love and for figuring out how to grow up with two parents who are social workers!

Rita Guthrie, a childhood friend, for encouraging me to write a book!

I appreciate **each author** in this book for their willingness to be interviewed and share their social work story with others.

Jennifer Bright, Bright Communications, for her guidance and wisdom in bringing this book to life!

About the Author

Hope Horowitz, MSW, LSW began her career in social services as a VISTA volunteer pursuing her passion to provide service to individuals and the community. Attending the University of Michigan School of Social Work provided the opportunity for her to focus  on community organization as she earned her MSW. She has enjoyed a distinguished career as a practitioner, trainer, and educator for over 42 years. She spent 23 years practicing in the Jewish communal field including 14 years as Regional Director for Central Region East of the B'nai B'rith Youth Organization and serving as Assistant Director for 9 years at the Allentown Jewish Community Center. She has been teaching at Northampton Community College since 2007 and is Professor of Social Work/Sociology.

Hope has served as a peer reviewer and facilitator for AmeriCorps State and National grants for several years. Her VISTA story was featured in AmeriCorps*VISTA 40th Anniversary Book, VISTA: In Service to America-Fighting Poverty for 40 years in May 2006. She has presented at various conferences including NASW-PA, CSWE, BPD, AASWG, SWAA, and international conferences. Since 1997, she has developed and taught a variety of approved continuing education workshops for social workers and other human service professionals. Hope served as Division Chair and Treasurer for NASW Eastern Division in Pennsylvania and served on the Board of Directors for NASW-PA. She continues to serve on the Phoebe Institute on Aging Educational Committee.

Hope received the honor of being named 2007 Social Worker of the Year for NASW Eastern (Lehigh Valley) Division. She was the first recipient of the distinguished Northampton Community College Dick and Pat Richardson Spirit Award in 2011 recognizing her continued commitment to service in the community through service-learning trips and projects related to Hurricane Katrina. Hope received the prestigious Lifetime Achievement Award from NASW-PA in October 2016. She continues to be passionate about teaching and providing global experiences for students and faculty.